PRAISE FOR

Ocean Rhythms

Kindred Spirits

"Surrender to nature and the pull of the sea and immerse yourself in *Ocean Rhythms, Kindred Spirits*. Let Nielsen's reflections, insights, and adventures spirit you away to a world of sea, sunlight, salt air, and self-discovery."

~ **Tom Poland**, *A Southern Writer*, Author of
South Carolina Country Roads

"Sheree Nielsen has penned another fantastic read with *Ocean Rhythms, Kindred Spirits*, capturing one of our family's favorite things—traveling to the beach with our pups! Stories involving a beloved sand-loving golden retriever, and a cat who expresses love by waking the author with a 'gift', prompted memory-filled smiles. In *Ocean Rhythms, Kindred Spirits*, Sheree's love of family, travel and pets is a most enjoyable read—whether you're on a sofa, hammock, or the beach!

~ **Kent Whitaker**, Culinary Author,
Barbecue Guru—Great American Grilling

"A journey through sea and land, this book inspires self-reflection and universal connection. A refreshing collection of personal essays!"

~ **Trina Sotira**, Co-editor of *Shifts: An Anthology of Women's Growth Through Change*, 2016 Next Generation Indie Book Awards Finalist,
2015 USA Best Book Award Finalist

"*Ocean Rhythms, Kindred Spirits* is a charming collection of moments and memories reminding us to value life's small blessings."

~ **Pat Wahler**, Author of *I am Mrs. Jesse James*

Ocean Rhythms

Kindred Spirits

AN EMERSON-INSPIRED
ESSAY COLLECTION ON
TRAVEL, NATURE, FAMILY AND PETS

For information or use of material from the book, please contact:

Ocean Spirit Photography, a division of Ocean Spirit, LLC
P.O. Box. 112
Wentzville, MO 63385

Library of Congress Control Number: 2018951828

ISBN: 978-0-692-14307-0
Cover photography: Sheree K. Nielsen

Cover design: Jennifer Quinlan
Author Portrait: Melissa Skidmore Photography
Book design: Country Mouse Design
Early Content Editor: Trina Sotira
Line and Copy Editor: Kelly Gamble, Joy Editing

SHEREE'S WORK HAS APPEARED IN ORIGINAL
OR SLIGHTLY DIFFERENT FORM IN THE FOLLOWING:

"Breakfast with the Queen"
—*Not Your Mother's Book on Cats*, and *Well Versed Literary Works 2012*

"Christmas Eve with the Cousins"
—*Solstice: A Winter Anthology*

"Island Girl"
—*The Eleutheran*

"Meet Jimmie McInnis—Bronze Star Recipient"
—*Proud to Be: Writing by American Warriors Volume III*

"Morning Delight"
—*Well Versed Literary Works 2014*

"Return to Folly Beach" and "Beach Dances"
—*Folly Current*

"Sweet Soles"
—*Well Versed 2018, Prose and Poetry*
FIRST PLACE FOR NONFICTION—ALL WRITE NOW! WRITER'S CONFERENCE, 2017

"The Dolphin's Dance"
—*Well Versed Literary Works 2015*

"The Edge"
—*The Abaconian*

"The Forecast Called for Rain"
—*Storyteller Magazine*
PEOPLE'S CHOICE AWARD, FIRST PLACE FOR NON-FICTION APRIL/MAY/JUNE 2010

"The Perfect Day"
—*Cuivre River Anthology IV*, and *Folly Current*

"Uncle Willie's Cabin"
—*Monroe County Illinois Suburban Journals*

DEDICATION

For Dad who instilled wanderlust in my soul through countless Southern beach vacations and fishing trips to the Great Lakes. I loved hearing about your time in the South Pacific aboard the U.S.S. Vestal during World War II. You're a man who can laugh at his own jokes.

For Mom who adored nature, gardening and cooking. I'll always cherish the memory of you tooling down the interstate in my brother's convertible while I was wearing the silky yellow floral scarf on my head, and abruptly losing it to the wind.

"What's gone is gone," was Mom's response.

To all the amazing people I've met through my adventures, the fur babies I've rescued, and my friends and family.

"I'd rather travel than be rich,
for to experience life, is the best part of living."

Sheree K. Nielsen

TO SOME OF THE PLACES I'VE LOVED

(Appearing in order)

Chesterfield, MO

Florida Keys

Jacksonville Beach, FL

Camp Whipolt, MN

Southport, NC

Kindred Spirit Bench, SC

Great Guana Cay, Abaco, Bahamas

Folly Beach, SC

Cotton Bay, Eleuthera

Sunset Beach, NC

Bimini, Bahamas

Sandy Cay, BVI's

Cayman Brac, Cayman Islands

Santa Rosa Beach, FL

Bloody Bay Wall, Cayman Islands

Millstadt, IL

St. Louis, MO

Sunset Beach, Eleuthera

O'Fallon, MO

Valmeyer, IL

Mississippi

Alabama I-65

Wentzville, MO

Middle Caicos, Turks & Caicos Islands

TABLE OF CONTENTS

INTRODUCTION

OCEAN RHYTHMS

7

KINDRED SPIRITS

99

AFTERWORD

177

"Every particular in nature, a leaf, a drop, a crystal, a moment of time is related to the whole, and partakes of the perfection of the whole."

~ Ralph Waldo Emerson

INTRODUCTION

Wednesday Awakenings

Wednesday, January 14, 2015, was a bitterly cold day in Missouri. With a dead car battery, my local automotive repair tech stopped by the house to jump start my Chevy Equinox. The technician suggested I drive the car at least forty minutes to avoid having the same problem again. I'd only been gone a couple hours running errands with my friend Peggy, when I returned home.

As I stepped inside the kitchen door, my two dogs and black cat greeted me with excitement. But an uneasy feeling filled my heart, as I spotted my sweet tuxedo kitty, Tripoli, lying on the wool rug in our dining room in the same spot where I rest my feet when seated at the table. I approached him slowly. There was no reaction when I called his name; no heave and ho of his breathing. Tripoli's silky black and white fur was still warm to the touch, but his lemon-colored eyes exhibited a fixed stare. I stroked his fur and began to cry uncontrollably. He was gone.

Grief gives no rhyme or reason—no warning. Crying outbursts know no sense of time, location or circumstance. Devastated by the loss of my friend, my unpredictable sobbing continued for days. The following Wednesday, on the one-week anniversary of his death, I cried off and on.

Wednesday, February 4 was different, though. In the quiet of the morning, as I lay in bed, I was startled by a loud male voice calling my name.

I wasn't sure if I was in the transition period between dreams and consciousness, but immediately, I sprang up, eyes wide open.

The ethereal voice sounded like...God's? Although I have no clue what God's voice sounds like, I thought it must be Him. The strong sublime voice was urging me, 'Wake up!'

Wake up now?
Wake up to my surroundings?
Wake up to life?
What was he saying?

I arose from our king-size bed, slipped on my white crew socks and worn cotton robe, and stumbled down the hallway to the kitchen. Two pooches and one cat followed close behind.

As I pushed open the sheer dining room curtains, the most magnificent yellow-orange sunrise radiated across the sky. I smiled. Peacefulness filled my heart.

Sauntering to the kitchen to prepare my routine breakfast of oatmeal and fresh raspberries, I eyed the resident gray squirrel, Bandit (named by me for the dark stripe under his eyes), on the porch. Inching his way down the wooden deck rail, he separated sunflower seeds from their hulls, munching on the meaty treat inside.

Seated at the kitchen table with my oatmeal, rye toast, and cup of English Breakfast tea, I noticed a pair of cardinals hopping across the deck outside our French doors.

I felt like God was telling me to 'wake up' and embrace the beauty around me.

The visuals of nature helped me forge through the rest of the week. I cried a little but remembered the beauty I'd discovered on that Wednesday morning.

Then on February 11, something happened in the wee hours of the morning—a strange dream.

In the dream, I awoke from slumber. The back door to our vacation home was open, and welcoming sunlight poured in. The hardwood floors of the hallway were cool to my bare feet as I shuffled into the living room, where my husband relaxed on a plush beige sofa.

I didn't notice our Australian shepherd, Sabrina, at first, but when she emerged from behind another sofa, a cat was riding her piggyback.

As I approached my smiling canine, I studied the cat's fur and color. His body, mainly white, sported light grey spots. The reddish-brown color of his head and face were separated by a white streak traveling from his crown to his nose.

Waking from the dream, I thought the cat reminded me of a parrot. The corners of my mouth upturned into a grin.

After breakfast, I scuffled down the hallway to the bathroom. Squeezing the Crest toothpaste tube, a tiny bubble formed, and floated upward. The small masterpiece remained airborne for what seemed like five minutes. I watched the bubble travel about the bathroom much like a hot air balloon adjusts to altitude. First up, then down, then sideways, toward the window, over the tub, and back towards me like an astronaut weightless in a space capsule. I stepped into the bedroom to grab my camera to capture a shot of the bubble, but when I returned it had disappeared.

Later in the afternoon, my young friend Rileigh and I ordered lunch at a local coffee house. When the server delivered my lunch salad, it

Tripoli in window

was drenched in dressing, rather than on the side, as I had requested. The server politely offered to prepare a second one. Upon his return, he handed me two wooden coin tokens for any coffee beverage and apologized for the inconvenience.

After lunch, we visited the Sophie Sachs Butterfly House, and observed more than twenty varieties of butterflies in a humid glass-encased botanical garden. The fragrance, the flowers, and temperature of the habitat brought back memories of my visits to the Caribbean.

Blue Morphos floated past us, just like the toothpaste bubble. Rileigh and I rested on the welcoming wood benches and observed the airy creatures in flight. My heart rate slowed as calmness filled my body.

We concluded the afternoon with a trip to a local bakery, The Cup, to stuff our faces with sweet delights like homemade chocolate cupcakes drenched in peanut butter cream icing.

Although the events of a particular Wednesday left a somber and melancholy feeling in my heart, I believe God's loving arms helped me realize Wednesdays are to be celebrated—whether through death, or a new life, or a change.

I believe that my precious three-legged fur baby, Tripoli, running free on Rainbow Bridge, would want me to savor all the good and positive moments that Wednesdays bring.

I decided that Wednesdays are 'get out of jail free' days—a break from the crazy world of stress.

I look forward to more unexplained sweet 'awakenings' in my life, and know that God always plays a part.

There's always an animal child that seems to connect with you, seeing right through to your soul, more than others. Tripoli was my 'heart' cat, and I'll always have the fondest memories of him.

How to read the book...

Ocean Rhythms uncovers the wanderlust in my soul, defining moments of clarity in my life, and when I experience nature's majesty whether blissful or extreme through beach and scuba diving adventures, and lyrical dances with creatures—dolphins, sharks, and sea-loving dogs.

Kindred Spirits reveals my strong connection to family, heritage, sweet childhood memories, beloved pets, and pleasant coincidences.

In these life journeys, I've found my own awakening—a universal beauty connecting every living thing on Earth to each other, as mentioned by Ralph Waldo Emerson in his ninth essay, "The Oversoul", and triggered by my lymphoma diagnosis in June 2012.

Since then, these essays and connections have taken on greater meaning—a higher purpose.

Life is constantly changing, and so are you. Use these essays as a foundation to link the universal beauty around you to your own experiences—every leaf, every drop, every creature, and with every being.

I hope you find yourself, and awaken the majesty of the Earth inside your soul.

OCEAN RHYTHMS

"Once you make a decision, the universe conspires to make it happen."

~Ralph Waldo Emerson

IN SEARCH OF MY KINDRED SPIRIT

Growing up in the Midwest, I learned quickly that my dad, a World War II naval veteran, longed to be near big bodies of water. Dad made sure Mom and I visited lakes or coastal regions in our travels, even if it meant taking several vacations a year.

May was spent lazing in the Florida Keys. Some days we'd swim at the hotel. Others, we'd fish off the old (now defunct) Seven Mile Bridge. Casting our lines, Dad and I donned colorful straw hats—mine, wide-brimmed with peach-colored ribbons, his, cool like Frank's Sinatra's. We even tooled around the crystal clear Atlantic Ocean on our rental boat fishing for snapper and pompano.

After a visit to Key West, the three of us pointed our compass in the direction of Jacksonville Beach, for a stay at Aunt Mary's. Days were spent splashing in the surf, beachcombing for shells, and catching crabs for the nightly boils.

In August, we headed north to visit friends, Bud and Mary, owners of Camp Whipolt Resort near Walker, Minnesota. Perched high atop a cliff, rows of cabins with vistas of Leech Lake offered a timeless view, and the water beckoned.

My best friend for the week was the couple's one-eyed golden retriever, Toby, who lost his eye in a dog fight. Most mornings, Toby would show up at our cabin, lifting his paw to scratch the screen door—his call for breakfast. Dad fed him savory bits—crispy fried bacon, hamburger, or even tater tots. Toby accepted the treats with a gulp, and a smile.

The two of us, young girl and dog, were inseparable. With boundless energy, we'd sprint down the two flights of rickety wooden steps from cabin to shoreline, and spend endless afternoons jumping over the rocks and playing in the water. I'd skip stones across the inlet, and wave at Dad fishing with his buddies offshore. Toby, would survey the shallow crystal water, and with back arched, launch himself airborne, like he was jumping on a trampoline, dive-bombing the water. With his mouth open, and his one eye keenly trained on a prize, sometimes he'd snag a minnow or bluegill. Toby repeated this process, again and again, with precision. Holding my stomach, it was difficult to hold back the laughter.

Hours later, the low hum of a boat motor nearing the dock signaled the return of Dad. With a red cooler full of freshly caught crappie and walleye in hand, Dad and his fellow anglers carried the 'catch of the day' to the fish-cleaning house. Curious, I'd position myself on an upturned minnow bucket inside the hut. The art of the filet commenced with Rapala knives, and fish scales flew like birds in flight. The filets, hosed off in long skinny sinks equipped with drains, were bathed in cool water, secured in Ziploc bags, and finally placed in a big deep freeze at Bud and Mary's cabin. Of course, we'd save a dozen or so fish for a cookout that evening.

While I felt at home returning each summer to these beloved getaways, I longed to discover my own 'old, yet familiar' place.

On a recent visit to my cousin Bob and Annie's in Southport, North Carolina, my husband, Russell and I found ourselves exploring nearby towns on days the couple had prior commitments. One morning, we set our course to check out nearby beaches. During our drive, a torrential downpour ensued, and we veered our Chevy Equinox into a parking lot with a wood gazebo at Sunset Beach. Grabbing our umbrella from the car for shelter, we walked the boardwalk to the soft wet sand. The waves were tempestuous, and the wind was wild. And I was drawn to this place.

We vowed to return to Sunset Beach in a few days, when the forecast was sunny.

As our visit with my cousins drew to a close, with a few hours before our flight, we mapped a course past Sunset Beach on the way to the airport. Steering our car into a parking space, we stopped at the same lot with the cute gazebo. Hand in hand we strolled the zig-zaggy boardwalk to the beach.

Minutes after stepping foot on the soothing sand, a young boy dressed in blue t-shirt and white board shorts surprised me by drenching me with a bucket of water. I felt like scolding him, but all I could do was chuckle.

The boy motioned for us to follow him. He led us under the weathered pier, where a thirty-something woman relaxed in a red webbed chair, with legs crossed, enjoying the shade.

"That's my boy!"

"He sure has a good arm," I said.

The brown-haired woman laughed.

"Where you from?"

"Missouri."

"You been to the Kindred Spirit Bench?"

"Nope," I answered, shaking my head from side to side.

The woman explained the Kindred Spirit Bench sat high atop dunes on Bird Island. It was a 35-minute walk due west from the last beach access at 40th Street along the shoreline—but well worth it. About forty years ago, someone who wished to remain anonymous, built the Kindred Spirit Bench. Adjacent to the bench, stood a mailbox filled with journals... notes and letters from visitors all over the world. The journals, collected each week by 'helpers', ensured the penned thoughts made their way back to the secret originator.

"Sitting on the bench," she said, "is the best view of Bird Island."

A salty tear trickled down my check.

"What's wrong, hon?"

"I'm a writer, and what you said just touched my heart."

"Well, then, you've just got to see it!"

On the flight back, thoughts about my conversation with the woman on the beach resurfaced. After returning home, I cancelled our next vacation, and rebooked a quaint beach house on Sunset Beach, North Carolina. One month later, my blue-eyed Australian Shepherd, my silver-haired handsome hubby, and I drove fifteen hours to our southern destination on a mission of self-discovery.

The Wednesday after our arrival, I connected with the Kindred Spirit helpers—a local author, Jacqueline, and her friend, Sandy. Jack, as her friends like to call her, supplied me with a bike for our trek to Bird Island and the Kindred Spirit Bench. After walking our bikes to the Third Street Beach Access, we hopped on for a leisurely ride. As we peddled, we talked. About twenty minutes into our trip, we sighted a black mailbox adjacent to a bench inscribed with the words "Kindred Spirit." We parked our bikes on the shoreline, using large scallop shells to house the kickstands, and hiked up the dunes to the bench.

I settled in on the weathered bench to rest from the ride. After a few minutes, I carefully opened the mailbox filled with journals. As I flipped the pages of the tattered notebooks, I found an entry from a young pregnant woman. Her baby was stillborn. Tape remained from an ultrasound photo, now removed. Another entry was from a young girl, and yet another from a grandmother...

I lifted my pen and scribbled in the journal,

"Dear Kindred Spirit,

I'm here with new friends Jacqueline and Sandy. Today, I watch as they carefully unfurl and hoist a flag for Memorial Day, in honor of all the veterans we've lost over the years. I call them the Kindred Spirit angels.

There are so many people, here, now, sharing the spirit. Everyone is connected to each other.

I pray my lymphoma never gets any worse than it is, my marriage grows stronger, and God watches over my animal children, family and friends."

A warm feeling embraced me. I now understood why this hallowed ground, frequented by residents and visitors alike, was so revered. Overcome with joy, I couldn't wait to share my experience with my husband.

Two days later, on a radiant Carolina morning, with canteens and cameras in-tow, hubby, the dog and I, made our journey down the beach to the Kindred Spirit Bench from the 40th Street beach access. Along the way, we took time to soak in the sights and sounds—seagulls soaring overhead, driftwood washed ashore, and children building sandcastles.

Arriving at our destination, my carefree animal child with the ice-blue eyes hopped up on one of the two weathered benches aside her Earth Mother. We cast a gaze onto the flat hard sand watching passersby carefully select seashells from the shallow tide pools. I turned my head to recognize a familiar symbol of bravery—the American flag—flying about ten yards behind the Kindred Spirit Bench. Set amidst a powder blue sky, nestled in the dunes, Old Glory was a sight to see today. Directly to my left, areas were roped off for sea turtle nesting and preservation. To my right, lay the jagged rocks of the jetty connecting the unpredictable ocean to the calm Intracoastal Waterway.

After slipping off his leather sandals, Russell opened the mailbox, and selected one of many notebooks housed inside. Reposed on the bench next to me, my veteran husband studied the American flag for several minutes, and then penned his thoughts in the journal. Finished, he returned the notebook to the mailbox, and gazed off into the distance.

"What did you write about, sweetie?"

"I wrote a letter to Wil. He would have loved this spot."

I felt a lump in my throat, as I held back tears.

Wil, my husband's friend, had a massive heart attack at age 34, leaving a wife, and four children behind.

In reverence, I bowed my head. I heard my dog panting next to me, and the sounds of waves crashing. Lifting my head, my eyes caressed the offing. Taking a deep breath, the salty air teased my nostrils. I knew I'd found my 'old, yet new familiar' place. With no doubt in my mind, I'd return again and again to this inspirational spot—this Kindred Spirit—with husband and animal children.

Our walk back was filled with excitement and emotion.

As I passed others on our walk, I'd smile and ask, "Do you know about the Kindred Spirit Bench? No? Well, let me tell you about it!"

Russell at the Kindred Spirit Beach

*"Never lose an opportunity of seeing anything beautiful,
for beauty is God's handwriting.*

~ Ralph Waldo Emerson

THE EDGE

A glimmer of Caribbean sunlight peeked through the white wooden blinds casting shadows on the hardwood floors in the blue room. Barefoot, I snacked on bran flakes from the comfort of a white wicker chair, and watched Russell dozing in dreamland. As he pushed the overstuffed pillows aside on the king-size bed and opened his eyes, I smiled in admiration. In a soft voice, I reminded him we needed to gather our scuba gear for today's dive.

After a quick cup of java, he arranged our dive equipment into mesh bags with wetsuit and fins on bottom, and primary gear on top. Snatching the bags, we lumbered down the stairs at the inn. Passing the pool, we chuckled when spotting the resident heron sipping his morning beverage of chlorinated water. Tossing our gear in the back of the golf cart, we puttered to the boat dock, taking in all the flora and fauna Great Guana Cay has to offer.

Dive master Troy greeted us at the dock where we handed him our gear, and stepped aboard his boat. Another diver, Ray, greeted us onboard.

The ride out to the dive site, The Edge, was a pleasant one. We passed Fisher Cay and Fowl Cay, both equally unspoiled Bahamian treasures.

Chatting with Troy, we discovered he's the father of two adorable girls and he proudly displayed wallet-size photos for our viewing. He grew up in Nassau and admitted diving has always been in his veins. From the age of 11, he worked weekends in his grandmother's shop learning the business and becoming skilled at his passion.

Troy killed the boat's engine, and dropped anchor near a buoy at The Edge dive site. Donning full gear and mask, I navigated aft of the boat, slipped into my teal fins and then jumped giant stride formation off the platform. Russell followed close behind. We gave each other the 'okay' sign at the surface, and agreed to meet on the sandy bottom.

As I began my descent, I released air in my buoyancy compensator, and dove headfirst like a dolphin in a ballet with the sea. A bath-like 82 degrees, the water visibility was exceptional. As the salty ocean enveloped my neoprene wetsuit, I continued to descend, remembering to pinch my nose on the way down. Clearing my ears, I heard a 'pop' and the pressure in my ear canals subsided.

I quickly glanced at my depth gauge which read 46 feet, and made eye contact with Russell on the soft sea bed. A friendly grouper greeted Troy and maneuvered around Ray, hubby and me, similar to a faithful dog declaring his hellos. The grouper stayed close to Troy giving us a seal of approval.

Within minutes, Troy gave the underwater signal for 'shark'—index finger and thumb at a right angle on top of his head. Russell pointed at a seven foot Caribbean reef shark, and a rush of adrenalin filled my body. The shark locked a gaze on me for what seemed like minutes, but was mere seconds. Swimming effortlessly in our direction, I noticed his magnitude. As quickly as he approached, he darted away. Hypnotized, I shook myself out of a 'shark coma' and resumed the dive.

The happy grouper brushed up against my side and persuaded me to pet him. I slid my hand across the fish's body, which felt like a slick coating of oil and silk. Afterwards, the grouper flapped his fins, and flaunted his plump lips—mimicking a woman with a recent Botox injection.

Again, Troy gave the hand signal for 'shark'. Russell, repeatedly tugging on my buoyancy compensator to get my attention, pointed out a ten-foot long black tip reef shark floating twenty-five feet overhead. I positioned the underwater camera and clicked off a quick shot. Troy cupped his stomach and then pointed to the shark's round belly, signaling me to 'swim up' and 'snap a photo'. I shook my head vehemently from side to side, wishing to keep my distance from the massive creature.

Russell snatched the camera from my hand and fearlessly ascended. He was eye to eye with her—as close as three feet away, in her personal space. I looked up, and against all scuba rules, held my breath. I exhaled...slow and deliberate. The two, captivated with each other, were suspended neutrally buoyant in the languid sea. My husband passionately snapped the shark's photo.

Long and lean, she slipped through the water in the company of two bar jacks that gave the appearance of the Christian fish symbol, gliding near her face. Four slits above her dorsal fin for breathing were visible, which sat in perfect alignment with her eye. There were several scars adjacent to her lower lip and a small gash above her fins. She was gracious as well as graceful. Hues of gray, violet and silver with delicate tones of a 'pale' bruised yellow blanketed her body. The shark, lovely as a dusky sunset over the ocean, hovered back and forth watching our every move. She seemed relaxed yet cautious near us.

The grouper swam alongside Troy and drew my attention. I waited patiently for another photo op. Troy motioned to the grouper with a curled index finger to come closer. Surprisingly, the fish understood the dive master's sign language. Troy cupped the grouper's face with his hands, smiled and kissed him sweetly as they gazed at each other with loving affection. Tenderly, he patted the grouper on the head and the fish scurried off.

After Troy released wheat bread stored in his buoyancy compensator pockets, the yellowtails went into a feeding frenzy. Flashes of white, yellow and silver spiraled around his body similar to a lasso, engulfing him in a Picasso-ish blur that impaired our visibility. After the feeding, I checked my air, which registered 1200 psi (pounds per square inch). The four of us headed back to the boat.

Enthralled by the marine life, I often lost track of time and forgot Russell was always nearby. Occasionally, I glanced back to check on my scuba buddy, and he'd flash me the 'okay' signal, putting my mind at ease everything was fine.

Russell motioned for me to come closer, pointed to our gauges, and visually checked our air consumption. Mine registered 750 psi. Sensing worry in his eyes, he grasped my bicep and swam swiftly in Troy's direction. Frenetically, I tried to keep up. Tapping Troy on the shoulder, Russell flashed my gauge mere inches from Troy's mask. He signaled 'okay', and I watched the tension leave Russell's body.

With the boat now in our line of sight, we visited a reef teaming with countless species of colorful fish. Yellowtails shadowed Troy recognizing him from a prior feeding. I spotted a shy gray angelfish with pouty lips, hiding in a rock crevice. She mustered up enough confidence to venture out. Steadying the camera, I set it precisely but was distracted when the welcoming grouper swam up to me eye to eye for attention. Stroking the grouper much like I would pet a dog, he flapped his fins in excitement.

Heading into the shallows, we spent idle time floating above the coral, investigating rock crevices, and completing a three-minute safety stop.

Ray and Troy were the first to ascend. Russell and I lingered in the warm seawater with prismatic rays of sunlight filtering from above. Relaxed, I floated neutrally buoyant for a few more minutes. I began my ascent fin-kicking upward keeping the silhouette of the boat and ladder in eyeshot. Beneath me, the grouper teased and circled Russell demanding personal attention.

As Russell climbed the rungs of the boat ladder, my watch read 11:16 a.m., and my dive computer logged forty-six minutes for the first site. We slid out of our clingy neoprene wetsuits, and took a seat on the bench in the sunlight. I offered the guys Altoid Tangerine Sours, and we compared notes about the fish life that piqued our interest.

Jumping into the captain's chair, Troy revved up the boat engine and jetted across the glassy water while briefing us about the next dive site, Tunnels. Intentionally, Troy rode the wakes of other boats as we sped through the water, causing the boat to bounce. I didn't care, and loved how the wind tangled my hair, and salty sea mist sprayed my rosy cheeks.

Troy paused for a moment and the corners of his mouth upturned in a grin like the Cheshire cat from *Alice in Wonderland*. "Oh, by the way, the black tip reef shark we saw was pregnant. The Caribbean was her mate."

Wide-eyed, Russell and I looked at each other in wonderment, grinning ear-to-ear.

Later, as we reflected on the events of the day, we found it hard to recall a more memorable day of diving.

We realized that today's blessings came in many forms—the friendly groupers swimming alongside us in harmony, the peaceful solitude and quiet of the deep, the sun's rays from above, and rare shark sightings of mother with child.

Photo credit: Russell Nielsen

"Live in the sunshine, swim the sea, drink the wild air."

~ Ralph Waldo Emerson

THE PERFECT DAY

Arms full, we toted our gear to the beach and found our personal space on the soft, comforting sand. Impatiently, I broke open the bag of cheddar cheese pretzels and quickly munched six or seven. Close by, a seagull, with no prior intentions of confiscating our food, waited patiently as I threw bird-size portions of the pretzels to him. He was quite a considerate bird, waiting quietly...not too close. The other birds were moochers—landing for the sole purpose of squelching our food. They received not a morsel for their devious efforts.

Russell and I walked to the water's edge, where we tested the temperature with our toes. It was chilly! He coaxed me, gently, just a little farther, until we were about sixty yards offshore. I spotted movement about ten yards out. Three bottlenose dolphins glided through the water, poetically surfacing, diving, and resurfacing in a synchronized ballet. They were for our eyes only.

After watching for fifteen minutes, we turned and moved gently through the water towards shore, returning to our beach pad. Russell headed southeast down the beach with the camera. I relaxed on the orange tater tot shaped pillow. When he returned, I asked what subject matter piqued his interest for photos.

He grinned. "The pier pilings from the old pier and the topless women."

Somehow, I didn't believe the comment about the women.

We sat for a while on the blanket contemplating paradise, taking in the dreamy views before our eyes. I decided to visit the northwest end of the beach and search for the 'perfect' seashell. The word 'perfect' in anyone's mind is what their perception of perfect is—incredible, beautiful, flawless, pristine, or impeccable. Perfect to one, is not perfect to another.

As I walked, I searched. There were thousands and thousands of shells, none alike, of every hue and texture. On that day, my perfect shells were the abalone, the knobbed whelk, the carinate dove snail, and the angel wing.

I began to think about my life and how we start fresh, strong and unblemished. Then along the way we pick up the sand and the grit, and sometimes we break, or we discolor, or people step on us becoming crushed underfoot. I felt like an 'old' shell—seasoned, weathered, but not worse for the wear. It had been a long journey before someone 'picked me' as the 'perfect' shell, but I am glad he did.

My thoughts turned to a tanned, seventyish man with gray hair in a red cotton bathing suit. He moved at a rapid pace from the sand dunes and then made a 90-degree turn and fell in line about thirty feet in front of me. The two of us walked in systematic order; I attempted to keep up with his pace. As we splashed through the water, I continued collecting, examining, discarding, and saving 'the perfect shells.'

Four pelicans were gliding overhead to my right in 'perfect' formation, like F15's on a mission—quietly, gracefully, moving through the air space.

I passed few sunbathers on my journey. With my husband now out of sight, I rounded the curve of the island. Glancing at my watch, I realized I had walked for 15 minutes. I looked back, then continued walking.

My tangerine neon bathing suit felt cool as the wind wistfully touched my skin and tousled my hair. I paid attention to the gray-haired man in the red bathing suit, walking at a 'perfect' militaristic pace in front of me.

I glanced at my watch again and thought, *Should I keep going? Is Russell getting worried? I'll just go a bit farther. I am a big girl. I can take care of myself.* My inner conscience justified my actions. *If any unsavory character approaches me, I'll defend myself with the 'perfect' sharp abalone I have here in my hand.*

The island shoreline took a decidedly drastic curve. I was now cognizant of small pools of water billowing parallel to the shore in front of the sea grass and dunes. This vision quickly conjured up an overwhelming spiritual feeling in me. If I could choose the 'perfect' day in heaven, it would be the dramatic underwater world in the morning and the brackish ocean air and seashore in the afternoon. I pondered what my perfect choice would be for the evening.

I paused, breathed, and surveyed. I took it all in—the dunes, the sea, the sand, the gray-haired man in the red bathing suit now nearly out of sight, birds flying overhead, and a tall tan adolescent man wearing a sunburst yellow ball cap as he walked near the dunes.

I turned around and walked the area where the water breaks on the sand, and I increased my momentum.

A sandpiper fell in place in front of me, replacing the gray-haired gentleman. We walked like this for quite a while. The sandpiper stepped quickly and gingerly, so as not to wet his feet, casually teasing the shoreline. I smiled, laughing silently as I follow.

I rounded the curve of the island. In the distance, I spotted a figure in a navy ball cap. Wearing white and gray print board shorts and sunglasses, he walked briskly with a front-to-back swagger of his arms. I knew this person. The good-looking man approached yet closer.

"Hi sweetie!" I said.

He responded. "Hey, I was worried about you (emphasis on the worried part)."

"Yeah, I thought you might be." I replied tenderly.

We walked back hand in hand. I shared with him my 'perfect' treasures cupped in my right hand. I gently set the treasures on the beach blanket. We ran giggling into the sea for a final 'cleansing'. I felt the water rush the back of my legs and inner thighs, as a crested wave broke. Hurrying to the blanket, I scribbled down my thoughts in my notebook. A leather-skinned, bleach blonde in a wrinkly pink T-shirt walked in front of me. She held a lime green koozie cup that surrounded a mysterious beverage and simultaneously balanced a cigarette, while bending, intently searching for the 'perfect' shell. I hoped she would find it.

Russell stroked the small of my back and touched the wisps of hair on my neck as I continued writing in my journal. He organized our beach items for departure, and shook the sand from the towels. As I penned my last few words, he sauntered to and from the water...pensive, wind blowing through his black silk floral Hawaiian shirt, salt and pepper hair secured in a ponytail, waiting patiently.

I soaked it up like Mom's white biscuit gravy...just one more look at Folly Beach.

I thought about the ocean in my soul, and the sand in my hair, and how lucky I was to have a perfect day in heaven, right here on Earth.

The Perfect Day

"We are all inventors, each sailing out on a voyage of discovery, guided each by a private chart..."

~ Ralph Waldo Emerson

RISKY BUSINESS

The air conditioning on our blue Chevy clunker we'd rented from a local, conked out shortly after leaving the Island School on Eleuthera. The unbearable temperature, displayed 100 degrees for the third day in a row, but wasn't nearly as bad as the humidity.

Equipped with an island map, we set out searching for elusive Cotton Bay Beach, a playground for the jazz set and elite back in the 1970's. There was Old Cotton Bay and New Cotton Bay. We didn't know the difference.

After a few wrong turns, the car puttered down a cracked asphalt road, past an unkempt golf course separated by a white picket fence. A weathered guard shack appeared where the fencing ended. Pulling up to the tiny building, we asked the attractive dark-skinned girl directions to Cotton Bay Beach.

Like a school traffic cop, she raised her arm and pointed due north. "Dat way," she instructed in island dialect.

We drove the scenic road, lined with palatial older homes complemented by magenta bougainvillea.

"Do you think we're going the right way?"

"Who's the navigator?"

"You are."

We gazed at splendid displays of Caribbean architecture encountered along our journey. The fragrant smell of frangipani and orchids dotting the private thoroughfare lingered long after we'd passed by.

Awakened by the distinctive floral smells, my mind suddenly became clear. Noticing the mature cotton trees, I realized we were smack dab in the middle of Old Cotton Bay. Stunning mansions oozed character and individuality.

The sweat trickling down my brow reminded me of how uncomfortably hot I felt.

"Pull over. I can't take this heat. And fix the air conditioning," I commanded.

Hubby steered the vehicle to the road's skinny shoulder. Pulling a Kleenex from the tissue box, I hopped out of the car.

"I'll be back."

I headed for a tall bush directly across from where we'd parked. Hoping it wasn't something poisonous, I perched my fanny on a hill, and let gravity take care of the rest. The strategic maneuver helped avoid contact with my leather sandals. I quickly pulled up my shorts and headed back to the car.

"The wires to the fuse box were loose. I just reconnected them," Russell reassured. "The a/c should work just fine."

"Thanks honey. You're the best."

Glancing to my right, I became completely enamored by a sprawling beige-colored ranch-style home. Floor-to-ceiling windows beckoned. The lawn, shaded by palm trees and blooming white yucca plants, complemented the landscape. A quick study of the backyard revealed Cotton Bay Beach approximately 100 yards away—the elusive puzzle piece we'd been seeking for nearly an hour.

Billowy, ornamental celery-green grasses divided the lawn from the shoreline, flanking a sandy path leading to the beach.

Happy and nervous, I propositioned my husband.

"Hey honey, pull the car over behind that hedge and park."

"What?"

"Let's have a picnic! We need to cool off and relax."

"Have you lost your mind? What if someone's home?"

"I'll check it out."

I casually strolled up the natural stone walkway to the home's front door, and touched my index finger to the doorbell. I waited. When no one answered, I turned right and continued along a path to the home's ocean side. Feeling adventurous, I pressed my face against the full-length windows and peered inside, cupping my hands tightly around my temples to block the bright Caribbean sunlight.

The furniture, covered with white sheets, and pictures placed carefully against the wall suggested no one was home.

With a newfound energy I skipped gleefully back to the car.

"C'mon. Let's have lunch!"

I removed the beach mat from the car's trunk. Hubby grabbed the sack lunch the gals at Cape Eleuthera Resort packed for us. We located a shady spot, wardrobed by soft mossy ground, welcoming us like a cool blanket. There, we spread out our beach mat.

The breeze of the swaying palm trees rustled through my moist hair—like young servants waving fans on Cleopatra. Russell removed our bounty from the paper bag, and placed the items on our makeshift table.

Our feast consisted of hoagie sandwiches, a cup of dill pickles, two bags of potato chips, two plastic spoons, and packets of mayo and mustard. And lots of napkins. I was a messy eater. A bottle of Lipton Iced Tea and a Coke quenched our thirst. We thanked the Lord for our meal, and Russell prayed for our safety during our island vacation.

As he lifted bread to his lips, I noticed his hands were shaking.

"What's the matter?"

"You're so transparent and trusting. What you see is what you get. When you looked in the windows of that house, visions of Pablo Escobar holding an Uzi stirred in my head," he admitted, "and you're the unsuspecting victim."

He justified his feelings by explaining that Eleuthera in the 1960's was a wild place—not for someone as naïve as his wife.

I thanked him for his concern.

"I didn't feel threatened. If something had happened, I would've talked my way out of it, or played dumb."

"I love you." He smiled with those big baby blues. "You scared me."

"Love you, too."

As I sipped my icy cold beverage, the offing behind my soulmate came into view.

Like the finest piece of gossamer, this vision was priceless.

Lissome palm trees framed a picture-perfect Cotton Bay Beach. The Caribbean Sea's effervescence sparkled like a precious aquamarine jewel against a cerulean blue sky.

As Emerson once said, "All life is an experiment. The more experiments you make the better."

Sometimes, life is more fun with detours—and finding Cotton Bay Beach was definitely worth the risk.

My day of living dangerously never seemed so complete.

Cotton Bay Beach

"...the great man is he who in the midst of the crowd, keeps with perfect sweetness, the independence of solitude."

~ Ralph Waldo Emerson

A BRONZE STAR

I met James "Jimmie" T. McInnis completely by accident. Strolling one fine morning on the Sunset Beach pier in North Carolina, my intentions were to check on my husband's fishing efforts and snap photos of his 'big' catch. I never made it to the end of the pier. Instead, I found another man more beguiling.

After spotting the gentleman's leather front-wheel drive wheelchair, I noticed his navy blue hat littered with countless medals. Bright gold embroidered capital letters emblazoned on the arc of the worn cap read, "Bronze Star". Directly underneath, "Vietnam Veteran" was stitched in red.

The veteran's cigar-hued face showed age behind cool aviator sunglasses and a neatly trimmed silver goatee. Two pens poked out of his light blue polo shirt pocket, and a silver medal hung around his neck. Wrapped tightly around his right wrist were four plastic bracelets—white (which said something about veterans), two black, and a red and blue two-toned sporting stars. I could only make out the words "Step Up For" on that one.

Jimmie, reading his newspaper intently, simultaneously was keeping an ever watchful eye on his fishing poles directly across the pier deck. I approached him, extending a hand and introduced myself. We exchanged names. Then I thanked him for serving our country.

After chatting with Jimmie for a while, I discovered he was a three time Vietnam War veteran with stints from 1967-68, 1970-72, and later again in 1972. He served from 1964-1980 in the Army's 25th Infantry Division, with base camp in Cu Chee, Vietnam. If anyone knows anything about the 25th Infantry you realize these guys were tough as nails, with nicknames like "Tropic Lightning", "Electric Strawberry", and the Cu Chi National Guard (during the Vietnam War).

Studying the veteran's cap, I recognized the shoulder sleeve insignia, red outlined by gold, with the shape representing a taro leaf native to the Hawaiian origin of the Army's 25th Infantry Division. A yellow lightning bolt symbol sat dead center of the insignia. This was pinned directly next to the Purple Heart.

He spoke briefly about how he received the Bronze Star and Purple Heart.

While in Vietnam serving near Vung Tau, a camp ammunition dump was blown up by a V-device.

As the dump exploded, Jimmie said, "I didn't stop to think—I was just called to action." He pulled four of his fellow comrades from the remains of the fiery dump.

Suffering bouts of PTSD in the past, he's been to the Fayetteville, Virginia Veterans Administration hospital for treatment. It's helped him sleep and cope better.

"The worst you can do is just not talk about it," he said.

Jimmie was duly awarded the Purple Heart and the Bronze Star for 'being a hero in action' in Vietnam—the medal closest to the Medal of Honor—from Lyndon B. Johnson.

His children have carried on the military tradition—one son is now retired from the Army, another son was promoted to Sergeant Major in the Army at El Paso, Texas..

By far, my favorite pin on Jimmie's 'cap of honors' is the silver Christian fish symbol which proudly displays bible verse, John 3:16. "For God so love the world that he gave his only Son, that whoever believes in Him, shall not perish but have eternal life."

Jimmie hales from Evergreen, North Carolina. One of life's greatest joys is fishing with his wife from the gray weathered Sunset Beach pier.

His secret to catching good fish—'fish bite' bait from Wal-Mart!

(Shush. Don't tell him I told you so.)

Jimmy on the Pier

"Nature is made to conspire with spirit to emancipate us."

~ Ralph Waldo Emerson

THE FORECAST CALLED FOR RAIN

It was late August 1995 and our 65 foot sailboat, the *Morning Star* of Blackbeard's Cruises, was preparing to depart the balmy island of Bimini after a much needed night of socializing at the Compleat Angler in Alice Town. It had been a rough trip, only two good days of diving out of six, because of the weather. Studying the flooded main street, a group of us decided to wade calf-deep to check local stores for rain gear in preparation for our journey home, which would be cut short by the rising storm front. Once secured with our protective garb, we garnered one final look at Bimini, sighed and waved our last goodbye. Despite all the unpredictable weather, I don't believe either Gilligan or Skipper experienced as much fun as we did.

We were a motley crew, 23 scuba divers and six crewmembers in all. Eleven of us hailed from St. Louis, with the remainder coming from Los Angeles, Philly, Chicago and Arkansas.

The *Morning Star* set sail early Thursday afternoon for Miami. The crew hoped an early jump on things would enable us to bypass the tropical storm that was headed in our direction. They were dead wrong.

We were smack dab in the middle of Tropical Storm Jerry. Gale winds and 25-foot wind swells pummeled the sailboat, as we huddled on deck in our rain jackets and shorts. The wind was biting cold and our jackets were rendered useless from the forces of the unforgiving sea. Our legs suffered the worst—exposed, red and goose bumped. Seems we had two choices—stay on deck and wait out the storm, or retreat to the comfort of the galley below and suffer the consequences of seasickness.

After four hours on deck in the torrential rain and nonstop pitching of the boat, I heard Craig, the first mate, say to Steve, the captain, "We just went an hour and a half in the wrong direction!"

If that wasn't bad enough, the fuel pump went out. After we digested this information, frustration set in. I was weary and chilled to the bone.

My throat ached from the group sing-along of show tunes and TV jingles in an effort to stay positive and to divert attention away from the gale winds and bitterly cold salty sea air. Shortly after we began singing the Gilligan's Island theme song, though, the crew became extremely agitated. They said it was bad *juju* to sing that song. When we asked what that phrase meant, they assured us that if we had to ask we didn't need to be singing that song.

Just shy of sunset, I was the first to retreat to the galley in an attempt to warm my bones. It was pointless to return to my bunk as I'd been informed the port side of the bow had major leaks. Once inside the galley, Maggie, our cook, greeted me. She opened my right hand and dropped wrapped treats in my palm.

"Suck peppermints...it will keep you from getting sick."

I quickly devoured six or seven. My tummy filled with the cool mint menthol that satisfied my soul.

The sailboat hit an incredibly large wind swell, which caused the stove to break loose from the wall in the galley. Out the window went our chance for a Bahamian dinner of lobster caught during a previous day of diving. Sipping my Constant Comment tea from a ceramic mug, I munched saltines and scones while seated on the wooden bench at the galley table. My eyes fixed a gaze on the 30-cup coffeemaker taking flight across the room. I ducked my head just in time, and thanked the Lord the coffeemaker had been empty.

Next, a tray of heavy silverware that included sharp steak knives soared above my head, as gracefully as the Flying Wallendas. *Hmmm, this is interesting*, I thought, casually sipping tea and nibbling scones, unfazed by the silverware circus.

One by one, my fellow shipmates retreated to the galley, unable to endure the whipping icy air. Soon all of us had gathered at the community table. We chatted, shared stories and maintained positive spirits, while our crew dealt with the concerns at hand. Our dinner consisted of saltines, cookies, instant mashed potatoes, cream cheese and microwaved SpaghettiO's.

If we craved peanut butter, we need not ask for it if the ship was rocking. The five-pound plastic tub was 'back at ya' as it slid from one end of the table to the other as if it were possessed. We laughed and cajoled, except for the mates who were reduced to drinking Sanka. Cranky, they desired fresh coffee. We laughed even more.

My fellow shipmates and I began to feel lightheaded and nauseated once the fuel pump fumes filtered into the galley. The crew hurried to fix the problem. Probably not our brightest decision, but certainly the easiest, was the choice to take a nap. Many of us with soaked sleeping quarters were offered a bunk-share with others who were willing to give up a portion of their personal space.

Hearing voices on deck, I arose from my short slumber and climbed the galley steps to survey the weather. Reaching the Port of Miami around 3 a.m., the vivid blue violet skyline blended with the tangerine hues of the early morning. The city lights of the high-rises glistened bright, casting reflections on the harbor. What a glorious time to reach land!

The intensity of tropical storms, can wreak havoc to anything along its path. In the face of adversity, and with the crew's teamwork, we weathered the storm's imminent danger, head on.

Hope, humility and a little dose of laughter helped everyone survive this tumultuous event and piece of nautical history called Tropical Storm Jerry.

The Forecast Called for Rain

"All life is an experiment.
The more experiments you make, the better".

~ Ralph Waldo Emerson

HAVEN'T I SEEN YOU SOMEWHERE?

Just east of Jost Van Dyke and shy of Green Cay, lies a tiny unspoiled island called Sandy Cay in the British Virgin Islands. One splendid October day, our Windjammer Tall Ship, *The Flying Cloud*, dropped anchor just offshore in the crystalline waters of the Caribbean.

Of the forty vacationers on board, twelve chose to go ashore for a beach barbeque and general lazing around. With towels and sunscreen in hand, we stepped down the ship's ladder to a smaller boat that would transport us to the Cay. The boat tender puttered slowly through the waters, allowing us to soak in our tropical surroundings. Once on land, the activity director, Patricia, and her crew set up the net and spikes for the beach volleyball game, and the picnic area.

Traveling solo, my bunkmates were three gals from Boston I'd met aboard ship. As newfound friends, we had a wonderful time snorkeling, basking in the sunshine, eating, drinking and playing sand volleyball.

The exotic island treasure dotted with palm trees, created a natural botanical garden and gently sloping beaches. Somehow, I knew this piece of heaven would be one of my favorites in years to come.

Steve, a lively honeymooner from Philly who had been dropping his trousers aboard the *Flying Cloud* most of the week, was anxious to organize a 'mooning' for the next boat tender arriving to take us back to the ship. Persuasive with a winning personality, Steve convinced us to partake in the challenge.

Steve lined up all the bronzed vacationers in a perfect row on the beach, coordinating bathing suit colors—reds next to pink and red-oranges, black next to gray. You get the idea. Even Monica, our blonde Swedish cruise director was persuaded to participate in the shenanigans.

"When I say boom, boom, boom, everyone drop your drawers!" Steve instructed.

Inching closer to shore, I spotted the boat tender that would transport us back to the *Flying Cloud*. With hand raised, Steve gave the cue to commence the depantsing. Within seconds—boom, boom, boom—twelve sets of bare-naked buns glistened on the beach. In contrast to our Coppertone-tanned bodies, our bottoms stood out like full moons on a clear night. The approaching dinghy of crewmembers' mouths dropped in disbelief.

Moored not far from the *Flying Cloud*, was *Caribbean Sol*, a sailboat. After our stellar performance, we spotted the sailboat's dinghy a few yards offshore. As the boat approached the shore's edge, and dropped anchor, two young couples hopped out. With cameras in hand, they strolled the white powdery sand beach. Had they perhaps captured the spectacular photo op that occurred a few minutes earlier?

Several days later, on my American Airlines prop flight from Tortola to San Juan, I struck up a conversation with several friendly tourists. One couple mentioned the fabulous time spent cruising the British Virgin Islands in their sailboat, *Caribbean Sol*. Fascinating ports of call were discovered just by shadowing the *Flying Cloud*'s course traversing the aquamarine sea. The couple recalled a memorable afternoon on their Sandy Cay boat approach, snapping photos of at least a dozen people 'mooning' on the beach.

"You sure look familiar" a handsome thirty-something gentleman with chiseled features remarked to me.

Grinning from ear to ear, I replied, "I was there that afternoon, participating in the organized beach event. I noticed your sailboat cruising the waters nearby."

The man's eyes grew large as his face turned a deep tomato red. Simultaneously, we both chuckled.

"Well, I'll just have to send you a photo of that memorable day."

"Cheers!" we both chimed with glasses raised, and toasted to a great vacation.

Haven't I Seen You Somewhere Before?

"Be not the slave of your own past.
Plunge into the sublime seas, dive deep and swim far,
so you shall come back with self-respect, with new power, with an
advanced experience that shall explain and overlook the old."

~ Ralph Waldo Emerson

THE DOLPHIN'S DANCE

Nearly four years to the day, my husband Russell and I stepped foot again on Cayman Brac—an island paradise about 12 ½ miles long. The Brac, aptly named by locals, boasted a rocky coastline, 140-foot bluff, and cerulean blue waters which gave way to some of the finest diving in the Caribbean.

I was anxious to reacquaint myself with the treasures of the deep. On my bucket list—exploring the everchanging reefs, walls, and wrecks. Little did I know my week on the island would be incomparable. It would be a life adventure.

For our first dive, our boat, *Big Sister*, dropped anchor off the northern shore of Cayman Brac. Divers readied their gear, attaching BC's and regulators to air tanks. After a thorough equipment inspection, everyone settled in on the metal benches or climbed up top to the captain's area in preparation for the pre-dive briefing.

Two tanned and toned dive masters, Craig and Susi, led our group for the first full day of scuba. After a quick survey of the underwater location, both were back onboard for a dive briefing.

With colorful markers, Craig highlighted on the whiteboard landmarks such as coral, sponges, marine life, and other areas we might choose to explore.

"Middle Chute and West Chute exhibit two sloping wall crests with a pinnacle, surrounded by sand chutes—a very special dive site—the wall crest beginning at fifty-five feet and dropping well below 3,000 feet straight down into infinity," described Craig. "The chutes have a cascading effect—similar to sand waterfalls."

Craig sketched one last familiar marine mammal on the board, and explained our group was in for a treat.

Shortly after Hurricane Mitch hit Honduras, Central America, in late October, 1998, a young male bottlenose dolphin was seen near Grand Cayman with a lone companion—his mother. The two sustained injuries during the storm—beaten up badly in the surf line. Not long after their arrival, the female dolphin's body lay lifeless, washed up on the shore. The male dolphin, left with a wound near his tail, longed for his matriarch and stayed close by in the Grand Cayman waters. After the summer of 1999, the young 300-pound dolphin, named Spot by Cayman dive masters, made Cayman Brac his home.

The dive staff chuckled and warned us to be prepared—Spot was quite a character!

Suited up with our gear, hubby and I walked aft on the boat. Side by side, we jumped giant-stride from the platform, keeping one hand on our regulator and mask. As we made descent, we cleared our ears by grasping our nose, blowing and forcing pressure to be released from our masks. Reaching the ocean floor, we hovered above a sand bank waiting for the rest of our group. A quick check of my depth gauge displayed 83 feet.

In the sand flats, our welcoming committee greeted us—Spot!

Within minutes, the playful dolphin bumped several divers. Our group formed an open circle with Spot as the main attraction. The sleek dolphin moved effortlessly—frolicking and cavorting, weaving in and around each of us, sometimes nudging, and always giving the okay to caress his silky gray body so warm to the touch.

The corners of Spot's mouth seemed to upturn into a grin. Picking up speed, he propelled his strong frame to the surface to catch a breath, and then dove head first, turning within inches of the sandy floor. A game of fetch ensued when Craig placed a twig in Spot's mouth. The dolphin dared anyone to snatch the stick—*a catch me if you can* attitude.

My dive computer beeped, signaling it was time for me to ascend. I gave hubby a "thumbs up" and slowly we fin-kicked towards the surface. After leveling off at fifteen feet, I grasped the end of the stainless steel boat chain attached to the vessel for a five-minute safety stop. Russell hovered neutrally buoyant in the waters nearby. The sun's brilliant rays penetrated the crystal clear ocean enveloping my neoprene wetsuit, as I patiently waited out my allotted time.

As I glanced at Russell, he appeared to be sinking deeper. I flashed the hand signal "to come up and level off." He pointed above me. As I looked upward toward the silhouetted boat, I noticed Spot with the heavy chain links draped over his beak-like snout. With my hand securely grasping the chain, the 7-foot long dolphin swung me up, and down, then up again. I smiled and enjoyed the ride! My husband laughed causing bubbles to escape at a rapid pace from his mask.

I garnered one final look at this magnificent creature before I continued my ascent. As I released the chain, Spot, with head tilted, squealed with delight. With soulful eyes, the dolphin gave me a quick wink before swimming off to harass other divers.

Back on the boat, fellow shipmates compared field notes about their personal interactions with Spot. Some were nudged or bumped, others admit caressing or hugging the dolphin, and still others withstood his merciless teasing.

Following a second morning dive, Big Sister revved her engine, and steered a course to our afternoon site—The Wreck of the Kissimmee, a Cayman energy tugboat well past her prime, deliberately sunk in 1982 to aid in the reef system. As the boat killed her engine near the northern shore, we recognized a familiar face portside.

Spot had returned for an encore. I clapped my hands in delight. The dolphin patiently waited at the surface for our group to re-enter the ocean's warm embrace.

We dropped quickly to the sea bottom, where visibility was excellent—as far as one's eye could see. While exploring the wreck's nooks and crannies, Spot lingered in the sand flats close by.

Swimming the length of the tugboat, we spent time inspecting vibrant macro life decorating the wreck, and gazing at peacock flounders and stingrays skimming along the sand flats. With camera in hand, Russell captured me sitting cross-legged near a hatchway entrance. I snapped a photo of him showing off his muscular legs and looking like Lloyd Bridges from *Sea Hunt*.

A short distance away, behind the shipwreck, a coral reef teamed with grey angelfish, yellow snappers, blue tangs and lionfish. Diligently, I searched for the elusive sharpnose puffer with angel-like fins and seductive eyes. Sadly, she was nowhere to be found.

Steadying the camera, Russell leaned in towards the reef for a close-up photo of a yellowtail damselfish. In my peripheral vision, out of Russell's sight, Spot inched closer. Hubby, unaware of the dolphin's presence, was thrust four feet to his left as Spot playfully side-checked his body.

Russell turned and sneered in my direction as if I was the culprit. Motioning to my right, hubby spun around. His frown quickly turned to a smile as he shook a scolding finger at the dolphin. Beaming, Spot sashayed his head back and forth emitting a quacking sound mimicking laughter.

Craig swam up and floated the dolphin a stick. Ready for another game of fetch, Spot retrieved it in seconds. Divers exploring the wreck lost interest and turned their attention toward them. After a few minutes, Spot released the stick and began spinning in circles. Enamored by the dolphin's presence, I realized how completely perfect this creature was—formed by God's hands.

Craig took a cue from Spot's lead and glided parallel to the dolphin, reeling in the cool sea water. Nuzzling belly to belly, their ethereal dance mesmerized onlookers—as graceful as Cirque De Soleil. The high-spirited dolphin squealed with delight. Craig stroked Spot's silky body as their act came to a close.

Nearing journey's end, we joined fellow diver Mike resting in the sand flats, watching his wife, Rosie, float above. As I relaxed, I reflected on the events of the day and the silly dolphin cavorting, twisting, and rolling in the tepid sea.

It was no coincidence Spot found his way to "The Brac". Some say several minutes with a wild dolphin is a gift. If that's so, forty minutes with Spot must have been a miracle.

Choosing a worn beige hammock secured between two winsome palm trees for a nice respite, I closed my eyes and reminisced about my newfound friend.

Spot's carefree attitude and childlike playfulness taught me it was okay to take risks, just as he did after the loss of his mother, setting a fresh course for adventure.

Stoic and gentle with keen intuition, I remembered the dolphin's smile, funny character, the gleam in his eye, and the bright white spot near his tail. Wise beyond his years, I learned quickly from this 'water angel' to enjoy life, laugh easily and love deeply.

Locals say Spot stuck around the Cayman waters for about a year, bonding and swimming with the dive masters of the Brac nearly every day.

Then just as unexpectedly as he appeared, he left—to discover new horizons, make new friends, and chart new seas.

Photo credit: Jason Belport

*"Adopt the Peace of Nature,
her secret is patience"*

~ Ralph Waldo Emerson

THE PILLARS OF HERCULES

Relaxing on the bow of the moving boat, I leaned back as the wind whipped through my hair and the hot Caribbean rays roasted my pale Midwestern skin. Heading to our second destination, we passed the famous Richard Noggin Rock, named by the locals.

Craig, our dive master, mentioned we were in for a treat—a well-kept secret and little known dive site along the Bluffs on Cayman Brace's northeast point. The boat slowed its speed, and I glanced up at the rocky cliffs jutting out of the sea. They must have been over 100 feet high! Jutting out of the shallower water near the bluffs, lay boulders that had randomly fallen into the sea. After motoring around the point, the crew dropped anchor on the back side of the Bluffs.

Craig mapped out the points of interest about "The Pillars of Hercules" on a whiteboard. A shallow site thirty to forty feet deep, there would be plenty of bottom time—maybe an hour to explore the dramatic pillar coral on this site, some sitting fifteen to twenty feet high from their base.

Donning my equipment over my sleek swimsuit, I jumped in giant-stride from the dive platform. The tepid water temperature felt invigorating on my skin. With only ten pounds in my weight belt, I dropped effortlessly to the sea floor. Russell followed close behind. The sun's shadows danced on the rocky bluffs below the surface.

While drifting along the crushed seashell bottom, in the distance, I recognized the regal coral described by Craig. Tall butter cream pillar spires swayed softly and reminded me of bottle brushes, flourishing with banded butterflyfish and hogfish snappers. Close up, their bristles were actually polyp tips that opened and closed. We floated slowly around the circumference of the coral and snapped several photos in this bath-like atmosphere.

Continuing our journey, we swam over a colorful palette of marine life—corals, sponges, spiny lobsters, and green-pink parrotfish. Keeping our distance, we observed the porcupine fish, typically a shy creature. If provoked, it would inflate for protection. In my line of sight was a yellow headed wrasse sporting two distinctive lines near the upper eye—beautiful eyelashes. Its body shimmered with pearlescent purples, magentas, and greens. Taking our time to inspect the macro life, Russell and I encountered translucent sailfin blennies, chameleons of their surroundings.

Serendipitously, I zeroed in on a pile of small pebbles stacked like a mini-mountain with a crater in the center. Was this an entrance to a fish house? Patiently, I steadied my movement and placed one hand in the sand, slowing my breathing. Previous experience told me this 'house of rocks' was the humble abode of a banded jawfish. I detected a small head, grayish tan in color, with bug eyes, peeking up through the entrance of the stones.

As the jawfish began to venture out, I readied my camera for picture-taking. Gradually, he poked his head out of the hole. Moving vertically around his home, he meticulously nudged the fallen pebbles back into place that I accidentally repositioned during my approach.

As a wave surge stirred up silt in the sea bed, the jawfish became more vigilant. Additional rocks from his abode fell into the sand. He diligently restacked them as a carpenter would take care to place bricks in building a new home.

Wondering where my husband was, I detected a figure in the distance. I fin-kicked briskly toward the person and found Russell sitting Indian-style with mask abandoned on the ocean floor. Heart racing, I sensed something was awry. Reassuring him, I touched his arm, then placed his mask in his hand. Russell positioned it over his head, and I soon realized the nose section sat on his forehead, while the goggle area rested on his mouth. I held back a laugh. He flipped the mask and correctly placed it, and exhaled through his nose.

Taking the stylus to my underwater slate, he wrote, "This was a test to see if you were paying attention."

With a flick of my wrist, I erased the slate and scribbled, "I'm sorry," and drew the symbol for a frown face next to it.

"Buddies should stick together," he wrote.

We removed our regulators for a quick underwater kiss.

Swimming side by side, we soaked in the cool blues and greens and fiery reds of the soft corals and sponges as the sun's summery rays lit up the surrounding landscape.

They say surprises happen when you least expect them. I eyed a tiny sharpnose pufferfish—my guilty pleasure. Elusive as the day is long, I'd never been able to snap a good photo of him as long as I'd been diving. His olive upper body showed a marked contrast to a white lower half—and the fish was a mere three inches in length! Teasing me with bright flirty eyes and puckery lips, he swiftly maneuvered his angel-like fins in and out of the boulders and the shallow's soft corals. Occasionally, he turned back to see if I was following. Weary of the cat and mouse chase, I gave up my quest for the perfect photo.

Russell and I completed the last minutes of our dive sitting cross-legged on the sea floor—observing. Silhouettes of snorkelers swayed above us, casting heavenly shadows as light auras emanated from their bodies. A check of my dive computer revealed our bottom time was approaching an hour. In close range, schools of midnight blue damselfish drifted by, flapping their neon yellow tails.

Resting on the sandy bottom, the eternal sea enveloped me with her outstretched arms. I took a deep breath, and my lungs filled with air. I exhaled—slowly and deliberately.

And I was happy to be one with nature.

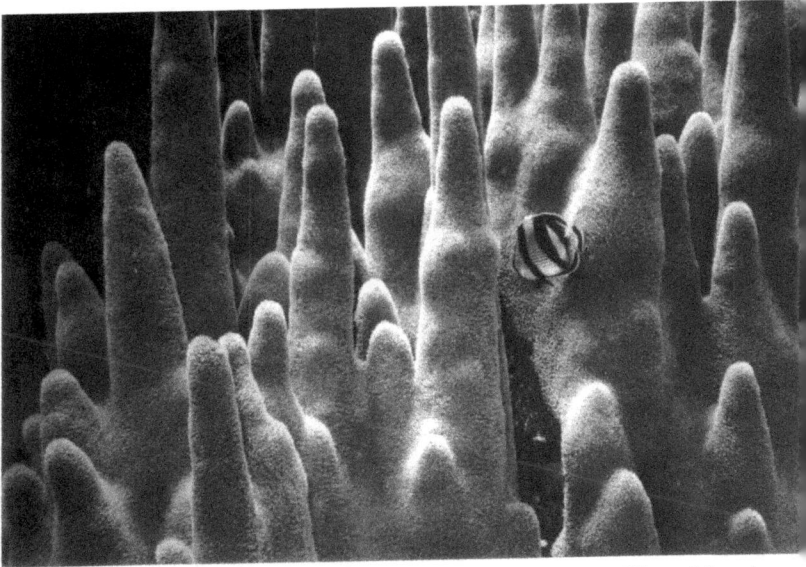

Pillars of Hercules

"Nature is a mutable cloud which is always and never the same."

~ Ralph Waldo Emerson

RETURN TO FOLLY BEACH

Like a child's curiosity to discover unfound treasures, my quest to reach the edge of the island on my last visit to Folly Beach became unfinished business.

With two cameras slung over my right shoulder—one digital and one DSLR—I began the trek at the point I left off last summer—the westernmost beach access. Arriving during low tide, the pools were brimming and plentiful. A sandy shelf formed close by the breaking waves and shoreline, with a two to three inch drop, and finally a tidal pool with snails and baby crabs.

My husband suggested to "leave it as I find it'—don't take anything that is alive." I honored his request to respect nature in its entire splendor.

Shuffling my way down the beach, I traveled on the sandy seashore just south of the tidal pools. Not far in the distance, I noticed an old tree, now driftwood, with branches reaching out to a cornflower blue sky and white-streaked cotton clouds. The image of a beach bungalow appeared in my head, with sounds of laughter, lazy days in the sun, peaceful ocean breezes, smoky barbeques at dusk and a warm crackling fire at night. I attempted to photograph the weathered tree, taking in the sea grass and dunes and the point where the ocean breaks into a marsh.

The beach beyond the driftwood remained a mystery to me. This place where wind meets calm, where rough meets smooth, where arid meets wet, a place of opposites yet similarities stirred up emotions of contentment and completeness in my soul.

Meandering a bit further, much to my surprise, I recognized the seventyish gentlemen that crossed my path the previous year. Sporting navy knee-length drawstring trunks and a Gorton's fisherman hat (last year clad in red), he stared in my direction. I suppose he thought I desired a photo of him. I did. Patiently, I waited until he lost interest. In an instant, I captured the moment in my camera's viewfinder, as he strode along the sandy ocean shelf at water's edge, amidst the breaking waves.

It only took minutes to wander to the tip of the island. I glanced at the tidal pools, too numerous to mention. The glistening water reflected from the sun hints of golden maze and beige gray in the late morning swelter with ripples that formed parallel to the sand similar to an Escher drawing. Mesmerized, I shot countless photos, alternating between cameras, so I could compare differences or similarities later.

Standing in the area where the ocean abuts the marsh, I heard the familiar, yet loud motor of a speedboat, even before viewing it. Once in my line of sight, the boat raced through the shallow waters. A bronzed pony-tailed brunette in a red sports bra, gym shorts and ball cap rounded the sandy area from the marsh to the ocean shoreline. She jogged at a rapid pace.

I paused to capture this visual photograph in my mind and swished my toes in the tepid salt water. On my journey back, a familiar face awaited me.

My soul mate returned to the beach with a shorter haircut than the previous year. Absent were his long locks of salt and pepper-hued luxuriousness. Others might have suspected that I had returned with another man. Signaling to him, I assured him I would be back in a minute. I glanced at my watch and realized I had been walking for an hour. Sprinting on the burning sand, I hurried to the car to grab a refreshing drink of water from the soft side cooler and once again, scampered down to the beach.

I observed my love inspecting and accumulating shells much like a young boy might select marbles or baseball cards. He was collecting them for me. I peered into the makeshift Wal-Mart shell collection bag and smiled with delight. Ecstatic at my response, he did a little hop-dance in place to show his enthusiasm. He carefully removed the shells for my approval. My favorites were all there—the whelks, the carinate dove snails and the angel wing. Placing the bag next to me on the sand, he decided to rove the sandy shelf adjacent to the tidal pools.

Directly in front of me, a mom donning a straw hat with black ribbon (similar to one you'd see in a Degas painting), sheer black cover-up and sunglasses, watched her toddler girl skimming the pools with mini boogie board in tow. Bending, stooping, splashing, the young child giggled with glee while making a fashion statement in her teal blue T-shirt, ruffled blue 'Coppertone' bottoms and a floppy pink cotton hat. Together, they examined the baby crabs and snails scurrying in the shallow pools of water. Enchanted by this scene unfolding, I ceased my picture taking, just for a moment, to embrace their spontaneity.

Removing her cover-up, the mom revealed a black bikini and a body fit for the suit—sleek, smooth and toned. Casually, mother and child strolled the shelf area between tidal pools where the ocean breaks. Spinning around, I noticed my husband was nowhere in sight. I thought to myself that he could take care of himself and chose not to worry.

A man in pink and brown board shorts carrying beach gear and coordinating brown vinyl chair passed and greeted me. I reciprocated with a big smile and "Hi, how are you?"

In my best lounging chair position, I stretched my arms and yawned, totally relaxed. My husband tiptoed up from behind and brushed a soft kiss on my ruby red forehead. Weary eyelids closed. I painted beautiful watercolor pictures in my mind, as I dreamed of celery greens, nubuck beiges, washed out whites, and cottony blues, colors representing the sea, the sand and the sky.

Nearing journey's end, my eyes lifted the final stroke of paint from brush to palette to canvas.

The Drifter — Return to Folly Beach

"Nature always wears the color of the spirit."

~ Ralph Waldo Emerson

CRAIG'S FLAG

I met Craig Hosner completely by accident.

As I steered my Chevy Silverado into a parking space at the Gulfview beach access, I noticed a fifty-something man wearing plaid shirt, jeans, tennis shoes, and rumpled hat, strolling with his small terrier on the sidewalk. Hopping out of the truck, I fell in line directly behind him on the way to the beach access. Dangling from his belt loops were two plastic bags—one bright yellow, the other, orange.

As I kicked off my worn black flip-flops on the boardwalk steps, I watched as the gentlemen untied both bags from his pants, setting them on the sand next to a large natural-made flag.

In my estimation, the flag spanned seven feet across and five feet long, and was a plethora of nature's phenomenon. If you looked closely, there were oyster shells, turtle nesting grass, palmetto cones, palm tree bark, pine needles and cones, driftwood, small shells (angel wings and scallops), and even feathers from brown pelicans, seagulls, terns and cormorants, making up the thirteen stripes of the flag.

Fifty sand dollars represented the fifty states of our nation—the white color signifying innocence and purity. The blue sail cloth served as the foundation for perseverance and justice.

It was awe-inspiring!

I noticed the man rummaging in the trash container close by, removing his treasure—a white plastic bag. Sauntering over to the flag, he leaned down and carefully placed the bag on top of an unfinished 'stripe', and sprinkled sand over the bag. Next, he emptied the contents of the yellow bag over the sand, revealing smaller shells.

"Are you the artist?"

"Yes, I am."

"I'm Sheree. Nice to meet you."

"Hi, I'm Craig," he said, offering his hand to shake.

"Do you mind if I ask you some questions?"

"Sure."

"Why do you place plastic bags beneath the shells?"

"It creates a buffer, and keeps the shells from sinking into the sand."

"Wow. Neat idea."

As we conversed, Craig told me he started the project last July with the oyster shells representing the first stripe of the American flag. His idea stemmed from the Christmas tree he created with oyster shells decorating his front lawn. The neighborhood kids thought his artwork was pretty cool, and slowly, the shells began disappearing off his property.

"I felt like the oyster shells could be put to better use. Hopefully, the kids won't steal them at the beach."

Craig admits he had to glue the sand dollars to the sail cloth because the smaller children were fascinated with them. Now, he carries extra sand dollars in his pockets, handing them out (with a smile), in case the children would like a souvenir.

"My Dad was a veteran."

"Mine too," I said.

Craig's inspiration for building the American flag—he just wanted to do it.

"There are smaller flags up and down Santa Rosa Beach....and hearts as well."

Gazing at me, the corners of his mouth upturned into a grin.

"They're beautiful!"

Incredibly, everyone seemed to know this man. Passersby shouted, "Great work, Craig!"

Even a young woman holding a small baby told me of Craig's sweet spirit.

"When Emily was born, he left a bouquet of pink roses on my doorstep."

As the sky transformed from golden maize to dreamy orange and lavenders, Craig, using the beach as his canvas, worked meticulously arranging the shells in perfect placement on the last stripe of the flag.

He says he's not finished.

Holding back tears, I watched as his silhouette set a patriotic tone, and the flag of natural beauty complimented the sun's glistening rays, embracing the ocean, the sand, and the surrounding landscape.

And it made me proud to be an American.

Craig's Flag

"Trust men and they will be true to you...."

~ Ralph Waldo Emerson

SWEET SOLES

There's an unspoken truth about shoes left at the beach. No matter how long you leave them on the boardwalk or in the sand, chances are, when you return from your walk or swim or kite flying, they'll be there waiting for you... eager to caress and soothe your tired, exfoliated feet, guiding you back to your house by the sea, Schwinn bicycle, or Jeep. Whether they're Teva black flip-flops, leather Birkenstocks, or the strappy gold metallic kind, sandals gather together for a shoe fest of their own.

I wonder what these shoes would say to each other if they could talk?

"Slow down!" or "You need a pedicure" or "Your soles are killing me!" or even "You're so soft and smooth".

They say you can tell a lot about someone by their shoes. I suppose the same applies for sandals.

I know mine are the 'comfort' Teva's—the longer they're worn, the more they conform to my feet. The fabric straps once ebony black, have faded to a pleasant midnight-purple, bleached by the sun and kissed by my toes.

Sometimes they require a good 'ole Dawn dish liquid washing after particles of sand get stuck in the cracks or they pick up smells from the beach.

Every time I slip on those flip-flops, they remind me of all the places I've visited, and countless adventures I've yet to experience.

Over the years, I've purchased a couple more pairs of sandals. But somehow, I end up choosing the seasoned black Teva's over all the others.

My husband says beach sandals remind him of the diversity in this world, and how each person, like sandals, can be different from one another. Some sandals have thick complex stitching or expensive leather. Others are as simple and humble as a molded ninety-nine cent pair of plastic flip-flops from the Dollar Store.

Eyeing those sandals lined up along the boardwalk steps, or

scattered in the sand, I realize people have chosen to trust each other. When we kick off our shoes, we leave worries behind, allowing the beach to invigorate, renew, and strengthen our minds and bodies. We're left vulnerable—open to sights and sounds, and even conversations with perfect strangers.

And just like our naked soles at the beach, we become one with each other.

Sweet Soles – Shoes on the Beach

*"That which dominates our imaginations and our thoughts,
will determine our lives and our character."*

~Ralph Waldo Emerson

BEACH DANCES

Before dusk, the beach rental owner busied himself sweeping sand from the white wooden chairs. Close by, my husband and I relaxed on the loungers, watching the motion of the straw broom as the man readied the chairs for tomorrow.

Off to our right, a group of six thirty-something gals gathered, each with a colorful Hula Hoop. A slender brunette dressed differently than the others, wore black stretchy hip hugger bell bottoms and a black bikini top. The ladies formed a circle on the sand. Much like a slinky moves down steps, they oscillated the colorful hoops over neck, chest, waist, knees and hips in a continuous motion until the circular toys dropped at their feet.

The sleek brunette mentored the women, effortlessly, rotating the colorful hoops, switching from hand to hand. Attempting this technique for themselves, some women displayed more success than others.

A forty-something attractive man dressed in a crisp polo shirt and tan Bermuda shorts sat cross-legged in a dark sailcloth chair near the gals while his faithful basset hound relaxed in the sand beside him. The two created a serene snapshot set against the Dreamsicle sky and the glistening sea.

Beer in hand, the man conversed with a musician-type donning long brown hair and wiry beard, a black skull emblem T-shirt, also sipping a beer. The musician's aviator sunglasses reflected the beach scene around him. Both men smiled with pride as they occasionally glanced in the direction of the ladies.

The captivating women drew in a constant stream of passersby. Some came to pet the basset hound; others attempted their hand at the art of hula hooping.

An inebriated shirtless young man in his twenties stopped to watch the gals. His face and chest were reddish purple—the result of too much sun. Already unstable, he picked up a Hula Hoop and swiveled it around his upper body in an attempt to keep it from dropping. The motion was not enough to make it stay in flight, and the hoop fell from the man's chest to the sand. Several more attempts were made, unsuccessfully. A cute tanned brunette walked by and remarked to him, "You have to keep the hoop *around* your spare tire!"

A ponytailed girl sporting a tank top and short shorts walked her pit bull a little too close to the basset hound. The frisky pit bull began wrestling with the other dog, attempting to pin it down. The rambunctious pair made me nervous.

The forty-something man seemed quite content, eyes affixed on the sultry women. The blood red sun dropped low on the horizon, casting shadowed outlines on the beach. Some long, some linear, and some triangular—each shadow depicting a person, a structure, or a movement.

An elderly woman petted the basset hound and the dog's ears flopped from side to side, as he sported a toothy grin.

"I'll be back in a jiff." I told my husband. Missing my two canine children at home, I meandered over to meet the dog and his owner.

"What's your dog's name?"

The gentleman replied, "Bobby Joe".

She was a sweet girl with soulful eyes, animated eyebrows and a winning personality.

As I conversed with the man, one of the women dropped her hoop and veered in my direction. I struck up a conversation with the two and discovered they were married. Admitting their love for the ocean, they've enjoyed the beach life for more than seventeen years. Whenever possible, they slip away to the waves to relax.

At twilight, the other gals lost momentum. One by one, they dimmed like lights on a stage, until one was left. The brunette with the sleek body undulated her hips to hold the hoop in motion. Similar to a belly dancer with sheer veils and tiny bells, she swayed gracefully in sync with the waves of the ocean. The musician-type cheered her on.

Purveying my surroundings, I recognized life embracing balance and movement all around me—evident in the kite boarder slipping down the shoreline, the sandpipers soaring overhead catching a wave of air lifting them higher, the hurried gait of a sunbather as she realized she had stayed past her allotted time, and the pre-teen girl gently bouncing her baby sister up and down.

Throughout my journeys, I've engaged in many conversations on sandy shorelines where the rhythm of life links us together. Everything, including the particles of sand on the beach shape the island down to the ocean carved shoreline to create this infinite and 'dance' we call Earth.

At the beach, we become like pieces of smooth multi-colored glass, washing away our sharpness and softening us around the edges.

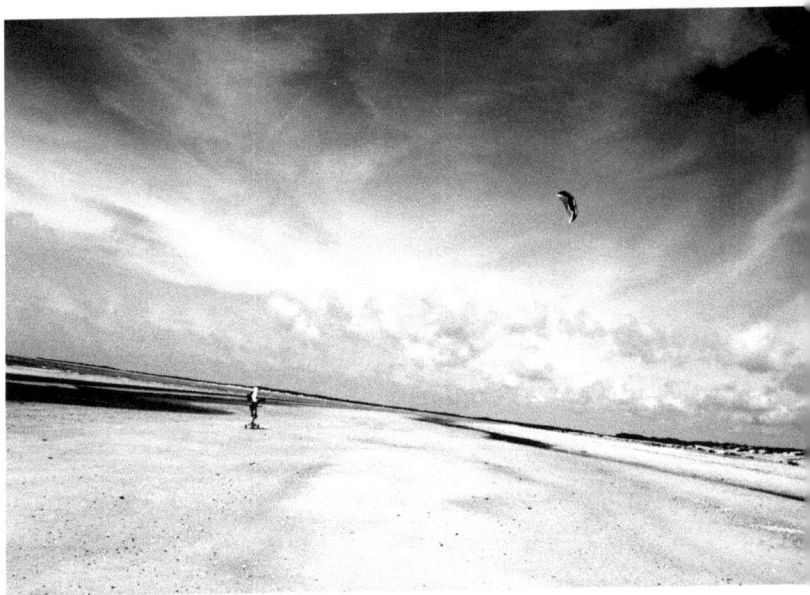

Beach Dances – Kite Dance

*"The lover of nature is he whose inward and outward senses
are truly adjusted to each other,
who has retained the spirit of infancy
even into the era of mankind."*

~ Ralph Waldo Emerson

LIFE ON THE WALL

Blood pulses through my veins. I envision loss of depth perception in my near future—peering over the ledge called Bloody Bay Wall, extending six thousand feet into watery oblivion.

The crystal clear sea is a bath-like 86 degrees; I wear a full-body dive skin for protection against abrasions. I self-baptize by jumping giant stride aft of the boat. Descending, I drop to forty-five feet to a coral head. Visibility is excellent—about one hundred feet in any direction. For twenty minutes or more, I swim easily, hovering and exploring the extensive marine life teeming in the reef—groupers, horse-eye jacks and turtles. Dive master Zam leads the way. Sheila, my dive buddy, and I follow close behind.

Anticipation builds and apprehension sets in as we reach the crest of the wall. I visualize the final scene in *Thelma and Louise*—women soaring over the edge of the Grand Canyon in their dusty blue '66 Thunderbird. Gliding near the wall's peak, fear of the unknown and exhilaration fills my body. My eyes open wide as an adrenaline smile fills my mask. Grabbing my underwater slate, I pen my exclamation of surprise with a popular four letter expletive.

Keeping the wall as a visual landmark, I fin-kick and swim downward. Pressure builds in my ear canals. Pinching my nose with my thumb and forefinger, my cheeks puff as I force an exhale, clearing my ears.

I check my depth gauge, which now reads seventy-eight feet. Glancing to my right, I study the blue abyss. An immense Caribbean reef shark, sleek and gray, appears unexpectedly out of the chasm. I inhale deeply from my regulator, and hold my breath—an action forbidden in scuba diving. I quickly remember to exhale.

The sky-hued abyss is omnipresent. Fifty feet away, the massive shark sways casually, hovering over the deep valley of infinity. As quickly as he materialized, the majestic creature slips from sight like magic into the distance.

Hanging neutrally buoyant, I investigate the vibrant display of life along the wall. I ogle rope corals and Swiss cheese-like barrel sponges in neon pink, cornflower blue, and red violet, making a mental note of the textures. The biodiversity of marine species is limitless— big-lipped blue tangs, lobsters and multi-colored queen triggerfish, all co-existing in harmony. I spot a purple transparent cleaner shrimp taking refuge in the curly tentacles of a corkscrew anemone. Living symbiotically, the shrimp feeds off the microorganisms as the anemone provides a safe haven for the tiny inhabitant.

I glide effortlessly observing the underwater world. Schools of Doctor fish and black durgon swim gracefully in a synchronized ballet moving vertically alongside the wall. Like *Alice in Wonderland*, I soak up the atmosphere like a gargantuan sponge. I spy brown and white spotted eels hiding in crevices, the greenish-pink parrotfish crunching on coral, and the zigzag movement of tiny sailfin blennies protecting their rocky homes built along outcroppings.

Turning briefly to look back, I'm amazed by the distance we've covered in such a short time. Slowly and deeply, I inhale and exhale from my regulator, sending bubbles to the surface. A feeling of freedom and enchantment overcome me, bewitched by the bountiful garden of splendor, and life on 'The Wall'.

Rolling gracefully as a dolphin, I flip upside down, and wave at my dive buddies Sheila and Zam.

They wave back.

Life on the Wall – Pink Azure Sponge

KINDRED SPIRITS

"The ornament of a house, is the friends who frequent it."

~ Ralph Waldo Emerson

UNCLE WILLIE'S FARM

Tires crackle from the noise of the gravel as my cousins and I travel down the long winding road to Uncle Willie's log cabin in Millstadt. Sorghum at least six feet tall, frame both sides of the country lane. In the distance, I catch a glimpse of the house. As we motor up, Alan and Gail bound out of their car.

Alan approaches an older man wearing blue jeans, a short sleeve shirt and an Oliver Tractor hat. The gentleman introduces himself as Korves and leans forward to shake hands with Alan.

"You're the Wagner's. We heard you might be stopping by today."

A red brick house with plantation style shutters sits adjacent to an old log cabin. The cabin is a sturdy structure—supposedly pre-revolutionary war era, sided with a light and medium grey shingle material.

We amble around the exterior of the log home. Korves explains the original surface was covered when he was a boy. The cabin's original brunette wood and pallid chinking is exposed near the base, more visible at the attic peak. The worn siding is falling off, and a weathered roof reveals shingles curled at the edges.

He offers a tour of the cabin. We step inside the kitchen, which leads to the living room unveiling the original stone double-sided fireplace painted stark white. We pass remains of a small-petrified lizard lying on the floor next to several boxes and trudge the steep steps to the attic. Dodging mud dauber nests attached to the ceiling boards, we purvey the attic. I examine the dark wood ceiling beams, looking closer at one with the Roman numeral "VII" etched in a slanted roof board. Korves mentions log homes arrived in numbered-board kits in days past.

Aunt Georgia glances up and reminisces about celebratory evenings spent in the log cabin. Weary from the night's events, she'd often fall asleep in a room off the main floor with her young friends. Uncle Willie and Aunt Hilda Wagner loved to entertain and opened their home to family and friends. Aunt Georgia recalls sitting on the stoop, watching the family churn homemade peach ice cream in preparation for a party. Another relative tells of how the Wagner boys slept in the attic. On wintry evenings while lying in their beds, they'd watch new fallen snow drift down through the rafters, sometimes touching their nose and eyelashes.

Aunt Georgia reflects on a time as a toddler when Grandma Kate (her mother) was stricken with pneumonia. The doctor prescribed *good food, rest, and warmth*. So off she went with Grandma to Uncle Willie's house for a stay until she was nursed back to health with tender loving care.

It's bittersweet how I remember my mom, now passed on, recounting stories about Uncle Willie's farm. Here I stood, a lifetime later, on the same ground that she found so familiar.

One anecdote Mom recounted about the farm, was when Aunt Hilda prepared her famous country breakfast complete with crisp homemade potato pancakes for all the cousins after early morning chores. Fresh and clean, everyone took up a seat at the long wooden table. Mom asked Eugene to pass the plate of potato pancakes, as well as the applesauce and sour cream toppings. Eugene just couldn't resist saying "Plop, plop, cow pies," while dropping a dollop of the toppings on Mom's pancakes. This comment had the cousins' bellies aching with laughter, finding it difficult to swallow their food.

Another tale Mom told involved an ornery bull. Uncle Willie raised cows and retained a bull for the heifers. Mom mentioned one day she was feeling a little feisty. The same day she and her sister Isabel, then teenagers, were dared to jump the fence to the field, probably by Eugene. Over the fence they gamboled. The bull charged the girls the minute their feet touched the cool green pasture and continued to chase them the entire length of the field! The bull's horns barely escaped scraping the seat of Mom's britches after she leapt back over the fence.

Exiting the homestead, Korves escorts us to the cellar entry through two slanted wooden doors on the ground. Inside, it's chilly, damp and musty. The soles of my dainty sandals adhere like a combination of honey and Play-Doh to the gooey gray mud. At the bottom of a set of wooden stairs lies a curved doorway consisting of interlocking pale bricks. Suspended with perfect engineering, the doorway appears mortar-less.

The farmer shows us the original barn encapsulated in the structure of a much larger building. Mahogany-colored planks run horizontally along antiquated walls. The wood appears sturdy and exquisite.

Korves is hospitable as we explore the old cemetery, a chicken coup, and other buildings. He supplied hay to the St. Louis Clydesdales for 26 years, and now delights in restoring Oliver Tractors, farms sorghum, and fancies collecting antique metal toys and Budweiser memorabilia.

Grateful for this experience with my family, I understand a little better this place called Uncle Willie's farm. I can only envision the playground this farm provided for my mother when she was a young girl full of dreams.

I have come full circle with my heritage. As the noonday sun warms me from the inside out, an overwhelming feeling fills my body. My throat starts to close and tears well in my eyes. Generations have passed, yet I feel the spirits of those that came before me. I am walking on precious ground. Oh, how I wished I had been around during that era, even just for a day.

I am thankful for the family who nurtures this piece of history and protects it with respect, love and admiration.

I look forward to next year's family reunion, learning more about my cousins, and Uncle Willie's farm.

And we won't need to call first—everyone will know the Wagners are in town.

Photo credit: Russell Nielsen

*"It is the quality of the moment,
not the number of days, or events, or of actors, that imports."*

~ Ralph Waldo Emerson

CHRISTMAS EVE WITH THE COUSINS

In memory of Georgia Lee Blasé
And Beatrice the Dog

Family tradition on Christmas Eve finds all of the cousins on Mom's side, including their children, gathered at Jackie's home in St. Louis. Guests travel from two counties to meet on the holiest of nights.

Arriving late, Russell gingerly steers me through a barrage of cousins in the kitchen. They quickly notice the neon orange and teal cast on my left leg.

"What happened?"

"I fell in a hole trying to help a dog."

I further explain on the first snowy night in December, a friend's Husky puppy accidentally wrapped its lead around an outdoor basketball pole. My husband and I attempted to unwind the pup's leash by marching in the opposite direction. After tromping in circles, I landed in a snow-covered depression made by the dog. A 'crack-pop' on the top of my foot was followed by a burning sensation. As I lay sobbing in the snow, the apologetic pup licked my salty tears. Turns out, I'd wear a cast for several weeks.

'There is never a dull moment' when all the cousins converge. One of us always has a story to tell, and tonight is no exception.

In the family room, I settle in on the loveseat. My husband assists in propping up my foot. The aroma of hazelnut coffee wafts from the kitchen and blends with the scent of cinnamon votives nearby. Cousin Leslie and I chat until summoned by Jackie to partake in the feast. Smaller children and those requiring extra help head up the buffet line. I guess that includes me.

Jackie displays a cornucopia of savory and mouthwatering food in her formal dining room—so festive it could be a photo spread in a woman's magazine. Without fail, Beatrice, the Border Collie attempts to sneak items from the table when the humans aren't paying attention. Cousins are strategically stationed as security guards, with hourly rotating shifts, to keep Beatrice at bay. This regimen is followed strictly. One year she successfully snatched a piece of roast beef right before my eyes and devoured it in seconds.

After dinner, I relax catching up on events in my cousins' lives until Jackie announces it is time for the gift exchange.

The gift exchange is exciting because each year, more and more of the cousins share in the giving. The gifts need not be expensive. The fun is in the opening. A flurry of green, red, and white tissue paper and embellished gift bags fill the room.

With the exception of Aunt Georgia, all of our parents have passed on. Wishing to make Christmas extra special for her this year, my husband and I give my aunt, a woman of faith, an etching of Jesus on clear glass about the size of a paperweight. She wraps a hug of approval around us after opening her gift.

Some of the cousins love to bake. Chris spends as much time baking as fellow cousins Andrea and Leslie. His wife Kim informs me he slaved away in the kitchen for nearly ten hours to prepare for this night! The results have paid off, as I sample some of the most scrumptious cookies this side of the Mississippi. The presentation is as important as the taste, and the cookies are displayed in colorful baskets and boxes. This year, my favorites are the crispy sesame seed, butterballs with mini chocolate chips and cinnamon, and the creamy dark chocolate truffles.

The first year Jackie held the celebration, in my typical absent-minded fashion I couldn't remember directions to her house. My husband and I were in transit when I phoned her.

"Jackie, what's your street address?"

"Why?" she asked.

"Isn't that party tonight?"

"Honey, you have your days mixed up. That was yesterday. Skip and I are just sitting down to dinner if you would like to join us."

"Umm, no, that's okay."

Going forward, Jackie made it a point to call me well ahead of time as a reminder the party was on Christmas Eve, not Christmas Day.

One of the more comical moments occurred a few years ago. While reaching over a candle centerpiece to grab an appetizer from a silver platter, I caught my navy Tommy Hilfiger sweater on fire. Due to possible low blood sugar, I was clueless anything was wrong. All I could think about was FOOD, FOOD, FOOD! The first to notice my burning sweater was Cousin Dan. Jumping up from the loveseat, he began slapping my arm. I thought to myself, why is he hitting me?

"Sheree, you're on fire!"

"Stop, drop and roll!"

I really should write Tommy Hilfiger a letter about his amazing product. Turns out, the unscathed sweater was flame retardant. (It still hangs in my closet.)

This evening, Aunt Georgia and Sue request I read a family story or two. Gathering my papers, I slip on my glasses. Before speaking, I peruse the various activities taking place. An enthusiastic group is engrossed in a trivia game. Their laughter fills the room. Several cousins partake in a heated discussion around the kitchen table exhibiting stern glances and facial grimaces. Others keep a watchful eye on Beatrice in the dining room as she paces near the plate of ham. I smile, proud to call them family.

As the evening comes to a close, hubby and I pat Beatrice on her head, and then bid my family members a fond farewell with kisses and hugs.

And just like the mailman, neither broken bones, nor fire nor snow could keep me from my cousins.

Christmas Eve — An Outdoor Winter Scene

"Be silly. Be honest. Be kind."

~ Ralph Waldo Emerson

ISLAND GIRL

I spotted her in the cool Caribbean ocean slightly off shore at Sunset Beach. Creamy beige wavy tresses hugged her body just below the neckline. Sand sprinkled round her eyes, nose and mouth complemented her cinnamon-complexioned face. A pink spot above her nose, about the size of a nickel, appeared hairless. She was 100 percent dog.

Moving slowly and deliberately, she pushed through the water towards me. An older girl, her snout was graced by whitish-beige whiskers. Droopy jowls highlighted her sparkling white teeth. Big brown eyes rounded out her face.

A robust golden retriever, she was definitely an Island Girl.

Approaching her gingerly, I offered my hand. She sniffed it with approval. Gently, I stroked the hair above her snout.

She followed me to a shady spot on the beach. I reclined on a white chaise in BarcaLounger-type fashion. She settled in on the sand, cooled by a swaying palm frond. Smitten with her (and she with me), we relaxed side-by-side.

Pulling the lounger to the water's edge, I submerged it, lowering my derriere onto the seat. Island Girl followed suit, crouching in front of me in the warm sea.

I located broken conch shells in the water and tossed them a short distance. Island Girl retrieved—in slow motion. No worries. She was on island time.

We frolicked liked this for fifteen minutes or more and made a good team. I was in charge of search, and she—in charge of recovery. With eyes open, Island Girl dove down to retrieve the large treasures, all the while blowing bubbles from her nose. With conch shell secured with her pearly whites, the canine, drenched in beads of salty water, delivered the mollusk—dropping it on the sand.

After the fifth retrieval, she exited the liquid playground, losing interest—her time better spent sniffing a particular spot on the beach, initiating a 'dig fest'. Using her snout as a shovel, she cast sand-sprays airborne, creating a considerable depression on the shore. Then she rolled in it! Covered from head to toe with the fine particles, Island Girl resembled a piece of caramel taffy dusted with sugar—so sweet!

In an effort to assist, I started digging, too. Intently, she examined and inspected my digging style and then joined in on the fun.

Island Girl lifted her head, cocked it to one side, and locked her eyes on mine. If she could speak, I am sure she would have said, "Well, aren't you going to roll in it?"

My body, exhausted from the sweltering heat, could bear no more shenanigans. Sticky sand laced my tanned skin like a coating of cookie sprinkles. I took a break on the lounger. Island Girl plopped down next to me, resting on the powdery beach.

Her features resembled Maggie's, our Chessie, whom we lost last October. The two shared similar traits—a gentle spirit, keen intuition and wisdom of a dog well beyond their years.

At water's edge, I slunk down deep into my chair seat in an effort to cool my legs and feet. Facing me, Island Girl squatted and plunged her hindquarters below the surface of the crystal, clear ocean.

I talked to her for a while like she was a great friend. Island Girl was the perfect listener. Those big brown eyes penetrated my soul.

I was in love.

Splashing my limbs in the bath-like atmosphere, Island Girl watched the motion of my hands and toes, studying every move.

After two hours in the Caribbean sun, my eyelids grew heavy. Ready for a nap, I bid my farewell, patted Island Girl on her head, and told her how much I enjoyed our afternoon together. Dragging my lounger to the sand, I gathered up my towel... and my husband.

Turning to look back, I caught a glimpse of the carefree canine— head poking above the water, gazing at me. I smiled knowing that just for a little while, she was *my* Island Girl.

A cute blonde in a black bikini hopped up from her lounger and meandered down to the shallows, approaching the dog. With Island Girl's approval, the young woman gently washed a light sprinkling of sand from the retriever's wet face, being extra careful around those big brown eyes. Satisfied with Island Girl's appearance, the blonde stroked the dog's flanks, patted her on the head, and rubbed behind the pooches' floppy ears.

A tear trickled down my cheek.

"I wonder if she has a home?"

"A sweet girl like that...how could she not?" hubby replied.

I counted my lucky stars for having met Island Girl on that glorious afternoon at Sunset Beach. That evening, I fell fast asleep with dreams of the golden retriever romping on the sandy shoreline.

Sharing lunch with my husband the following day, a warm hand touched my shoulder blade.

"Enjoying yourselves?" a man's voice inquired.

"Yes."

"Hi, I'm Stephen Kappeler, the General Manager," he said, offering his hand to shake.

"Everything's great, but who owns the pretty dog we met yesterday on Sunset Beach?"

"That's my girl, Lucky."

A sense of relief filled my body.

"I'm glad. I was worried my husband wouldn't let me take her home."

"She's a great dog. Loves the water."

As Stephen walked away, I told hubby how happy I was my newfound friend had a good home. Thankful, too, she reminded me of our Maggie.

And so *lucky* to have met an authentic Island Girl named *Lucky*.

(The Kappeler's own Lucky and for years managed Cape Eleuthera Resort and Yacht Club on the island of Eleuthera in the Bahamas. Stephen said that many guests found Lucky an attraction in her own right on Sunset Beach. She loved small children and enjoyed visiting with them. If she got sandy from the beach, she headed home and stood by the hose to get her rinse. Lucky is still making new friends today on her current island home, Treasure Cay in the Bahamas.)

Photo credit: Maggie Kappeler

"It is not length of life, but depth of life."

~ Ralph Waldo Emerson

THE FIX-IT MAN

The previous owner left our newly acquired home in shambles. Food swept under the dirty kitchen carpet, torn window screens, clogged sinks, and grease fire stains on ceilings were areas begging attention. Many of our close friends graciously volunteered to assist in the clean-up.

Even my Dad got in on the act. Family and friends called him Joe. He excelled at everything from pouring concrete patios, building custom barbeque pits, puttering on cars, to deep-frying homemade doughnuts.

As clean up commenced, chores were delegated. Jean washed filmy windows until they were squeaky clean, while Mary scrubbed tubs and toilets. My hubby and our friends, Mike, Tina, and Sue covered the walls and woodwork with fresh paint, giving the interior a new look. Debbie and Steve chucked odds and ends left behind by the prior owner, while I vacuumed and sanitized the carpet.

Built in the 70's, the kitchen required a complete overhaul. Dad and my husband's friend, Chris, demolished and removed the chipped particle-board cabinets. The two men, wearing protective goggles, equipped with electric power tools and crowbars, were on a mission, and nothing would get in their way!

Our curious black and tan Shepherd mix, Butch, was rambunctious due to all the activity. Clumsy puppy paws scampered into the kitchen to observe Dad and Chris. Underfoot while the men worked, Butch barked, insisting on supervising. The frisky canine caught Dad's attention. Reaching into his jeans pocket, he magically produced a liver treat which Butch quickly gobbled up. Joe's love for dogs was evident as he patted the puppy's furry head and massaged behind his floppy ears. Giving the pooch a nudge, he sent Butch on his way. The dog's tail swaggered back and forth, like a pendulum.

Upbeat tunes filtering from the radio lit up everyone's face. To further lighten the mood, Tina painted a white stripe down Butch's back and on his puppy pads. In no time at all, Butch bounded throughout the house, leaving a trail of white paw prints like a guilty culprit sprinkling evidence at a crime scene.

Dad, quickly recognizing my stress, scooped up Butch and set him down gently in a bucket of soapy water. He bathed the puppy with his weathered and gentle hands. Hands—aged by the sun from years of casting his fishing reel into placid lakes. Hands—arthritic from working the soil in his vegetable and fruit garden. And when Dad had washed the last bit of paint off the canine, he wrapped Butch in a fluffy terry towel, to wick away the bath water.

As the day wore on, with much of the cleaning and repairs accomplished, I checked items off the to-do list. With the cabinet removal complete, Chris took a break while Dad readied the grill for the pork ribs. Of all of Dad's talents, he was known best for creating the tastiest barbeque west of the Mississippi River. His homemade concoction revealed just a hint of teriyaki, mustard, and honey in the sauce—along with a few secret ingredients.

He chose hickory starter chips which gave the meat a woody flavor. The aroma wafted through the windows and casually teased the tips of my nostrils.

After the ribs were roasted to crispy perfection, I set out blue polka-dot paper plates and napkins on the kitchen counter. Friends and family filled their plates with the savory ribs, smothering them with Dad's secret sauce.

As I passed through the living room, my eyes were drawn to a scene unfolding on the sun porch. Two men relaxed across from each other at the white wooden table. Chris, in his late twenties, was fixated on Joe. No doubt the experienced angler was telling Chris how *the big one got way* or some World War II navy story. Chris sat captivated, frosty bottle of brew in hand, occasionally breaking out in bouts of laughter, his face resembling a red beet.

Upon closer inspection, I noticed a one-inch ring of barbeque sauce smeared around the perimeter of Dad's mouth. His sticky fingers grasped the ribs as he sunk his teeth into the meat, causing sauce to drip, drip, drip onto the paper plate. I couldn't tell if Chris was chuckling at my Dad's infant-in-a-highchair look or at *what* he was saying. My father rather enjoyed laughing at his own jokes.

Later, as the bright tangerine sun touched down on the horizon, one by one, my friends garnered seats on the porch. Gathered around Dad like fireflies to a mid-summer night sky, they chuckled as he spun tale after tale, all the while savoring his scrumptious barbeque—pausing only to lick his fingers and tilt back a beer.

From a distance, I watched, mesmerized. A warm feeling filled me. The laughter and camaraderie of that evening will forever be embedded in my mind—a cherished memory.

In my late twenties at the time, I already knew I had the coolest Dad around.

Dad went on to fix other things for me—like the garage door frame I backed into with my silver Pontiac Firebird, and the kitchen outlets I fried due to overloaded circuits.

And when Butch died unexpectedly due to a stomach issue—Dad mended my broken heart with some kind words and a loving embrace.

As he lay stricken with liver and stomach cancer in his hospital bed, Dad insisted he *"knew some people in high places"* and would help me *"fix"* my jobless situation. His networking skills paid off. The day my father left this world I was offered a full-time position at a telecom company where I spent fourteen years.

Funny, intelligent and generous to a fault, my Dad, the Fix-It Man, had a profound influence on how I lived my life.

Be wise, be humble, be smart, were the lessons he taught me.

But above all these—be a better person.

Photo credit: Gladys Klemites

"As we grow old, the beauty steals inward."

~ Ralph Waldo Emerson

THE OKEECHOBEE VALMEYER FISH FRY

Cousin Sue makes eye contact and waves from under the weathered rust colored roof of the metal pavilion, as we veer our car into the gravel parking lot at Borsch Memorial Park in Valmeyer, Illinois. I smile at Sue, and wave back.

My cousins are all here from Grandma's side—the Wagner kids—first, second and third cousins and Aunt Georgia. Cousin Gail grabs my hand and whisks me off to reintroduce me to the rest of the Wagner cousins.

We reminisce about a reunion held back in the late 1960's at Jackie and Norm's house in Piasa, Illinois. Perched on a sizeable piece of property, their house was surrounded by shade trees, overlooking a gorgeous lake, which made it a perfect venue for a gathering of our family.

I remember that day well. Gail's dad, Eugene, concocted a plan to round up four or five of us pre-teen kids, corral us into one of Norm's boats, and paddle to the middle of the lake. Eugene looked quite fashionable rowing, wearing a seersucker shirt, khaki shorts and a white Styrofoam dealer's hat with a playing card directly in front. Nearing our destination, Eugene jumped up dead center in the boat and sang his best rendition of "99 Bottles of Beer on the Wall" while sipping a cold, frosty Budweiser. Yes, he could carry a tune.

We giggled uncontrollably from Eugene's antics, tears streaming from our eyes. His balance was rocky at best. Several times, we were certain he was going to take a nose dive into the lake. Inevitably, the bottle of beer seemed to steady his frame. With outstretched arms, he utilized the drink like a trapeze artist balancing himself with a pole. As Eugene regained his footing, singing resumed.

After a few more laughs about the good times, I quickly wrap up the story about Eugene, as the thought of delectable fare pops into my head. I scurry to the food table.

They don't call it the Okeechobee Valmeyer Fish Fry for nothing! Fried crispy fish and frog legs are the order of the day. My eyes dart from the baked beans with dark molasses and thick bacon, to the green pea salad drenched with mayo, the cucumbers and onions in vinaigrette and the corkscrew pasta salad. I stop directly in front of the blackberry cobbler that calls out 'taste me'. I stack the flimsy paper plate high with palatable provisions until it is entirely covered. Happy with my selections, I saunter over to my soulmate and take a seat at the picnic table. I quickly devour the savory delights. Yum...comfort food.

At the table next to ours, cousin Jackie shares photo albums of past year reunions that include invitations and the fragile sign-in sheets. Vinyl pages, buckled and yellow, encase the faded nostalgia. The oldest albums are difficult to view—some of the photos have melded into the sleeves. Flipping through the pages, I am thankful she chose to document our history.

Pictures of Mom and Dad appear in the albums; she in her late forties and he in his early fifties; both hamming it up for the camera. My hubby quickly compares Mom's similarities to me—same goofy smile, long legs, auburn hair, and the poochy stomach. I am my mother's daughter and proud of it.

The 60's and the 70's were a simpler time. Picnics, birthdays and holidays called for celebration. Families cherished relationships—and food. Mom's roast beef in mushroom gravy and Dad's honey teriyaki ribs were mouthwatering. Dessert was homemade German chocolate cake. No emails, no cell phones, no computer—just the face-to-face interaction with people you love. Even the reunion invitations were elaborate, detailed and handwritten.

Years have come and gone. Compared to the huge parties of the past, this one seems small, but intimate. As we grow older, the dynamic of the reunion has changed with loved ones that have moved or passed on.

We aren't as young as we used to be, but the Wagner's still have the quick wit, wisdom and stories to pass on to the next generation. And I still have enough energy to get up and cut another slice of that blackberry cobbler.

Blackberry Cobbler from Okeechobee Valmeyer Fish Fry

"The Earth laughs in flowers"

~ Ralph Waldo Emerson

THE MIMOSA TREE

On a stretch of I-65, thirty miles north of Birmingham, rolling hills are confettied with Persian Silk mimosa trees, each more beautiful than the next. Their pink blossoms and fern-like leaves, stir memories of my childhood growing up in the 60's on Meramec Street in South St. Louis. My first swing set sat in the shade of a mimosa. Pushing toward the sky, I swung to and fro, cooled by the swaying feathery leaves, and calmed by the flower's intoxicating scent. Sometimes the oriental blooms dropped and tickled my feet while swinging.

The mimosa, my parents' favorite tree, reminded them of the South—good times and family vacations in beach towns and fishing villages along the coast in Mississippi, Alabama and Florida. They planted a mimosa to keep its beauty and those memories close.

On occasion, Mom pinched the pomesque blooms from the tree and bobby-pinned them in my white-blond hair. I remember, at the tender age of four, topless, wearing pink flip-flops and beige capris, with flowers in my tresses, I felt like a tanned Tahitian beauty.

As my body grew taller and stronger, so did the tree—outstretching light brown branches to protect me as I laughed and played with friends. Sometimes we'd throw the tan colored pods that had fallen from the tree back to the sky, pretending they were helicopters.

When my parents sold their house on Meramec Street, I was devastated. Dad's company moved to St. Charles County, and so did we. Seventeen at the time, I was about to start my senior year in high school. My best friend abandoned me for a guy, and I had no friends in our new town of St. Peters. That summer, I was bored out of my mind.

Seeing my frustration, Dad insisted on planting a mature mimosa. The tree embraced me through my dating years. Gentle breezes from its branches felt peaceful as Mom attempted to have "The Talk" with me about boys. Too bad I had already heard all about 'the birds and the bees' from my older cousins.

When I did bring boys home, the strong mimosa provided a safe haven for conversation, and sometimes, kissing.

Hummingbirds and butterflies sipped the flowers sweet nectar. The tree fanned lacy shade for family celebrations on the patio—barbeques, birthday parties, surprise wedding showers and finally, Dad's wake. Mom sold the house shortly after.

I miss both trees.

My husband and I attempted to grow a mimosa seedling shortly after we moved in our house on three acres. It required attention and tender loving care. I suppose we were too busy trying to grow grass, pour a concrete patio, and select stylish bedroom furniture rather than be concerned about that little mimosa. It withered and eventually dried up—it's leaves in a permanent slumber. My husband gave it a proper burial by plowing over it with the riding lawnmower.

Never have I seen more mimosas clustered together on any stretch of highway than I did passing near the Purple Heart Trail in Alabama on that magnificent summery day in July.

Maybe when we get home from our Florida vacation, we'll plant another mimosa tree. The silk flowers can make a happy mess on our deck. It would only be right.

Mimosa Tree

"Insist on Yourself. Never Imitate."

~ Ralph Waldo Emerson

BREAKFAST WITH THE QUEEN

As the toaster springs forth my perfectly tanned pumpernickel bread, I sense a fat black presence in my peripheral vision. It's Midnight, our cat.

Over thirteen years have passed since my husband rescued Midnight one snowy evening in November. He noticed her as she lay trembling in a pool of motor oil under our car outside his favorite coffee shop. Dull and sticky, her fur coat was atrocious. Heaven knows how long she had been hiding under cars. Conveniently, our vet was across the street from the coffeehouse. The microchip beneath her skin revealed the owners left no forwarding address, and no phone number. A possible prank, maybe? A black cat purchased for Halloween, shunned after that scary night.

With the intentions of fostering, we brought her home until she could be placed with a suitable family. I wasn't fond of female cats. Firsthand experiences with friends and neighbors reinforced my fear of their bad temperament and furniture destruction.

Recommended by our vet, a degreasing was in order for Midnight. She and hubby bonded as he washed away her troubles and past lives with Dawn dishwashing liquid. Confined to solitary, she spent ten days in the master bathroom to clear up fleas and worms. She 'did her time' gracefully. Sitting pretty, she chatted with birds and squirrels through the two picture windows. Inquisitively, she watched as I applied my morning makeup. Hubby always conversed with her while showering and that seemed to make her happy.

We introduced Midnight to the rest of the animal family. It took a couple of months, but with her persuasive personality, she managed to easily dominate two male cats and two female dogs. And us. The street kitty blossomed into royalty, and we were all under her spell.

Midnight is currently invading my personal space as I lift the black ceramic cover to the butter dish. She loves butter. A guilty pleasure she picked up after months of observing her canine stepsisters Sasha and Maggie beg for the scrumptious treat.

Ever watchful, the motion of my hand lifting the knife to butter to bread causes a vocalization as she anticipates the ritual that occurs every morning. Breakfast. Midnight nudges me affectionately, as I slide the buttered bread onto a plate and place it on the kitchen table. She leaps counter-to-counter to reach her destination. Spoiled, she manages to position herself front and center, hoping I won't notice the dogs.

Here she sits displaying pink 'Her Majesty' bling (complete with crown) jingling from a magenta and gray collar complimenting her coal black fur. Plumped, primped, properly postured, lips pursed, she is prepared to pounce on the slice of pumpernickel if not offered to her pronto!

Midnight is not persnickety about her carbohydrates, be it rye bread, scone, muffin or sourdough. It is imperative; however, the bread be generously dripping in butter, the sweet cream kind—salted or unsalted. Don't serve her margarine or a cheap imitation—she knows the difference.

I lay a morsel before her. She inspects it briefly to ensure the entire portion is covered with her favorite fatty substance. As she daintily crunches the savory sustenance, the butter's exquisite quality melts with acceptance on her taste buds. She waits for another. And another. When her tummy is full, Midnight sashays toward her throne, the soft comforter of the guest bed, where she seeks solitude.

She is the epitome of a queen. And what the Queen wants the Queen gets.

And the Queen likes her bread and butter.

Midnight the Cat

"To know even one life has breathed easier because you have lived. This is to have succeeded."

~ Ralph Waldo Emerson

ROOFTOP TO THE BASEMENT

The Humane Society male cat area housed a jungle gym of sorts, enclosed by floor-to-ceiling fencing. Cats of all sizes and colors leapt in fits of pent-up anxiety. All but one. Serene and grand, he posed in the midst of all the chaos, tapping his tail like a pendulum. His short white fur displayed black markings on his back and head. His black crown sported a white separation, similar to a barbershop quartet singer. They called him Oreo. Uncanny as it may seem, with the shape of his face, parted hair and key lime eyes, he reminded me of my Dad. Reincarnated. My Dad hated cats.

The butter-hued wrinkled comment card attached to the cat's cage indicated "One year old". Personal remarks from Oreo read, "Mom and Dad gave me up in the divorce." Tears welled in my eyes. I couldn't imagine anyone giving up this beautiful animal.

The volunteer asked, "Would you like to spend time with him in the playroom?"

I nodded, "Yes."

Seated on a wooden bench, I reached over to stroke his soft fur, and his purr-motor kicked in. I was in love!

Phoning my husband, I informed him we were the proud parents of a cat! Unable to find a carrier, the volunteer rounded up a cardboard box for transportation and punched holes in it for air. Oreo complained the entire ride.

Once home, I gently placed the box on the floor of the garage near my husband who was staining woodwork. Cautiously, Oreo hopped out of the box and hid behind the drywall propped up against the wall. A couple of hours later, he journeyed from his hiding space, and the adventures began.

We renamed him Rory Gallagher for the rockin' blues guitarist of the 80's, befitting his cool personality.

We knew he fit in when Sasha, our Husky mix puppy and Rory became fast friends. Inseparable, they'd wrestle on the sun porch almost daily. As Sasha grew older, Rory hitched a ride through the house by attaching himself to her underbelly, wrapping his paws around her midsection like a koala baby.

As Rory and I bonded, his affection for me blossomed. Taking a seat on my pillow at bedtime, he'd positioned his soft underbelly around my head like a fur hat—his low purr lulling me to sleep.

Our screened sun porch overlooked a one-acre lot, common ground and fields. On crisp mornings, I shuffled barefoot onto the porch. Newspaper and coffee in hand, Rory pranced behind. I cherished our time together. Balancing on his back legs, he'd place his front paw on the window frame and curiously survey the antics of the feisty blue jays. At dusk, he scampered to the porch to listen to the cricket's song.

On evenings my husband returned home late from a band gig, Rory and I tiptoed down the porch steps to the center of the yard. Sitting contently on the concrete patio, the baby soft moonlight calmed my soul. On several occasions, streams of bright light jutted across the midnight blue sky.

"Rory, did you see that?" I'd say smiling.

Cooing loudly, and tilting his head in my direction, it's almost if Rory knew what I was saying.

On lonely nights when my husband never came home, Rory was there—comforting me, and licking away my salty tears.

Years later, I remarried. Suffering through a round of allergy shots, my second husband was determined to make me happy. Rory and my new love became good friends.

Asleep one wintry evening, I awoke abruptly with Rory hovering over me with an unidentifiable object in his mouth. As Rory dropped the item on my chest, I felt it move. Love overflowing, Rory had presented me with his prized possession—a live mouse. I flung the comforter off so fast the mouse took flight across the room. Eek! This similar situation would play out several more times over the next few years. Rory became a skillful mouser.

Aging gracefully, Rory enjoyed stretching out in the guest bedroom— the warm sunlight casting a rainbow of hues on his white and black fur. He loved to watch butterflies and woodpeckers outside. Nimbly, he'd balance on his back legs and position his front paws on the windowsill to get a front row seat of nature. When a stray cat, Scooby, adopted my husband, he became buddies with Rory. The two cats spent their days snuggling on the white beach rocker.

Days when I ironed, Rory enjoyed listening to me sing, "Don't Worry, Be Happy", as I turned up the volume on the radio. The louder I sang, the corners of his mouth upturned in a grin as he rolled on the carpet.

Rory was my sunshine.

Shortly after his twelfth birthday, Rory's breathing became shallow and he refused to eat food. Concerned, I made an appointment with the vet.

The prognosis—a heart condition. Countless trips to the veterinarian and a specialist were necessary to drain excess fluid, check blood levels and reevaluate medication. The side effects caused Rory's weight and energy levels to plummet.

Most days Rory hid in our bedroom closet on a pile of blankets. Venturing out one evening, he curled up on the dog pillow in the living room. Scooby joined him as if sensing Rory was suffering. When Rory shivered, Scooby pressed closer. Retrieving a blanket, I gently placed it over the two of them. After phoning the specialist, and describing Rory's condition, I advised his kidneys might be failing.

Still wrapped in the blanket, I carried Rory in my arms to the car for a trip to the animal hospital. My husband, who was driving, stopped to buy a soda at the local convenience mart. For a brief moment, Rory crawled from the warmth of the blanket to see what Daddy was doing. Placing his front paws on the dashboard, Rory perched his back legs on my lap and peered through the car window, watching Daddy move throughout the store. Rory stepped back lightly into the comfort of the blanket as hubby climbed back into the car. For a few seconds 'old' Rory was back.

The somber mood matched the scraping noise of the worn wiper blades across the windshield.

Holding Rory snugly, I whispered in his ear, "It's okay. If it is too painful for you to go on, just close your eyes and sleep." I planted a kiss on his cheek, as a tear dropped from mine.

Arriving at the hospital, I cradled Rory, and reluctantly surrendered him to the arms of a technician. The clock read 10 p.m. as the technician attached an IV to his frail body. Keeping him for observation, the doctor suggested we return the next morning.

Leaving him behind broke my heart.

The rain pounded our car window enroute to the hospital. Fifteen minutes into the journey, we received a call. My precious Rory had passed. My face flooded with emotion, felt similar to the downpour ensuing outside. "Kite", a U2 song was playing on the radio. The words from the song mentioned how life should be fragrant, from the top of the roof to the basement.

In a small, bare hospital room, Rory lay lifeless on a cold steel table. We stroked his frail body for the last time and bid goodbye to our sweet friend.

He made our lives fragrant...rooftop to the basement.

Rooftop to the Basement, Rory in the Wheelbarrow

"Give all to love, obey the heart."

~ Ralph Waldo Emerson

MY MORNING DELIGHT

In memory of Scooby,
who entered this world with a roar
and left with a quiet whisper.

In the stillness of the early morning, the owl is who-ing and the morning birds are chirping softly. Daylight peeks through the blinds casting tiny sunbeams on the carpet. Comfortably snuggled beneath cotton sheets, my hubby and I enjoy the cool breeze that envelops the room as the ceiling fan moves air downward. Eyes still closed, I feel four small paws walking on me followed by a gentle nudge on my forearm.

Awaking from slumber, I smile at my little friend. With every purr, I feel the beating of his heart. With every look, I see the love in his eyes. With every touch, I sense the wisdom and the gentleness in his feline soul.

He has grown sweeter with age. Brushing his gray and white tail against Daddy's back, he simultaneously kisses and head butts me on my upper lip.

"I love you Scooby".

My husband still in dreamland (thinking I am talking to him) answers, "I love you". Only Scooby knows the truth.

As I shuffle through the hallway in my pink fluffy slippers, Scooby shadows behind, mirroring the gait of a seasoned thoroughbred. I settle in front of the computer, and he poses himself next to me on a storage box.

Gently, Scooby preens and cleans his velvety fur. Satisfied with his handsome looks, he rubs the edge of the desk with contentment. He studies the movement of my hands as I click away at the keyboard and gives the desk another brush with his cheek.

Scooby's long white whiskers are sparser than they were fourteen years ago when he was a rambunctious kitten who flipped on light switches, chased wadded paper balls, and bit human ankles. As a youngster, he managed to jump with great agility straight up at least six feet to reach his favorite 'people viewing spot'—the entertainment center.

I like this new Scooby—a lover, not a fighter. As much as I enjoyed the eager and arrogant kitten he once was, I now savor the graceful and affable Scooby he has become.

Like the tortoise, and not the hare, with wide-eyes he saunters off to discover new places and things.

That's my Scoobity Do—wouldn't know what to do without ya.

My Morning Delight

"It's not the destination, it's the journey."

~ Ralph Waldo Emerson

THE RIGHT CHOICE

Of the five families that filled out an adoption application, we were the lucky ones. The director of St. Louis Aussie Rescue blessed us with the good news saying that our profile and love of dogs was a great fit for Sabrina.

The high-energy canine quickly won her way into our hearts. Bonding immediately, we settled into a routine, which included morning walks to familiarize her with the bucolic neighborhood.

One blissful autumn morning, Sabrina and I experienced sensory overload while meandering down the gravel path. Trees were shedding their delicate leaves, squirrels were foraging for nuts, and woodpeckers were doing what they do best—pecking. The strokes of a heavenly paintbrush inspired a canvas of rich fall colors.

During our stroll, the whipping wind tossed my hair into an unkempt mess. Bundled up in a teal Henley, Bermuda shorts and a bright yellow rain slicker, I felt a chill travel down my spine, even though the sun was shining. Sabrina's natural warmth was provided by her weather-resistant silky coat.

Turning left from the gravel path placed us on the sidewalk of the main road. A spur of the moment decision lead us to Nancy's house. Sabrina and I first met Nancy while out on a walk. Nancy, clad in gardening apparel, was tending to her native Missouri plants. We realized we shared a common thread for all things nature, and our friendship blossomed. Today was her birthday and we planned to surprise her with a dragonfly photo my husband snapped with his new Nikon camera.

Spotting Nancy in her driveway, I bid a joyful "Good morning!"

As she approached, Sabrina jumped up eagerly to greet her, giving her hand a birthday-lick with a soft puppy tongue. Nancy didn't own a dog but anticipated our morning visit and rewarded Sabrina with a yummy liver treat hidden in her coat pocket. Sabrina graciously accepted the tasty delight, and then gobbled it down.

After we chatted for a while, I wished Nancy a happy birthday, and handed her the pretty envelope with the photo tucked inside. Card in hand, she hopped into the passenger side of her car. Bob, her husband, sat in the driver's seat.

Walking a bit longer, Sabrina and I attempted to cross to the south side of the road. Bob unexpectedly stopped their vehicle in the center lane directly in front of us, rolling down the window.

"The photo was beautiful! Do know what kind of dragonfly it was?"

"I haven't the slightest!"

Bob informed me the fragile creature was a Halloween Pennant. How appropriate, I thought to myself. Halloween was just around the corner. I must have flipped through our portfolio of nature pics three or four times, always coming back to the photo of the interesting insect. It was amazing that I picked this photo, and almost uncanny that Bob could identify it.

I smiled and waved goodbye to Bob and Nancy as they maneuvered their auto out of the center lane of the parkway.

Pacing ourselves, Sabrina and I managed to reach Bear Creek subdivision within five minutes. There, we met Lucky, a lean and muscular German shepherd, led by his silver-haired sixty-something owner. The gentleman and I struck up a casual conversation about our dogs.

He believed Lucky was a puppy mill puppy. I nodded, having the same suspicion about my little girl. Meant for breeding, Sabrina had been confined to a kennel most of the day with rare opportunity for exercise or affection. At only two-years old, she was already a mother to a litter of pups—possibly two. Certainly, no life for a dog.

Lucky's owner and I spoke for several minutes, comparing information on rescue dogs. The silver-haired gentleman, both amicable and sweet, was smitten with his companion Lucky. As Lucky glanced up at his human partner—tongue hanging sideways out of his mouth and tail wagging to and fro, it was obvious the feeling was reciprocated.

Eventually, the pooches began to get restless, so we wrapped up our conversation.

"Have a great day!"

"You, too!"

With Sabrina by my side, I carefully crossed the parkway, looking in both directions for oncoming traffic.

Turning up the gravel road, Sabrina smiled at me with undying affection. So playful, she danced and trotted showing off her keen agility. Spinning in four full circles without stopping, this crazy canine 'walked herself'—grabbing the lead with her jaws, shaking it vigorously back and forth; my cue to get my butt in gear and keep up with her antics.

Approaching our driveway, I waved to Jerry, our next-door neighbor, working in his garage. Sabrina tugged me in his direction. Casting a glance up at Jerry with her iceberg blue eyes, the pooch balanced on her back legs, hopped up and nudged his hand, followed by a friendly lick. Jerry obliged by gently rubbing behind the canine's ears.

He noticed how Sabrina stayed close by my side when we walked. Jerry said it looked as if I had made the right choice. I agreed. This smart Aussie came a long way since her rescue six weeks ago.

Like Olympic runners, we sprinted across the lawn together towards the house. Out of breath, I clicked the door opener for entry into the garage. Stepping inside the kitchen, the spicy aroma of a quince-scented candle lingered.

I reflected on the morning.

Was it by chance I selected the delicate photo of a Halloween Pennant for Nancy's birthday card? Was the silver-haired man and Lucky placed in my path that morning to create a special bond? How fortunate were Russell and I to be Sabrina's forever home?

Coincidence? Maybe.

I believe unexplained coincidences happen all the time, even when you least expect them. The Lord is always guiding us, helping us through the day, giving us choices—hoping we make the right ones. We just have to listen. I happened to make the right choice with Sabrina.

As I pen this, my sweet baby girl dog sleeps on the blue wool rug beneath my feet.

Stay out of her way when she dreams. She kicks hard!

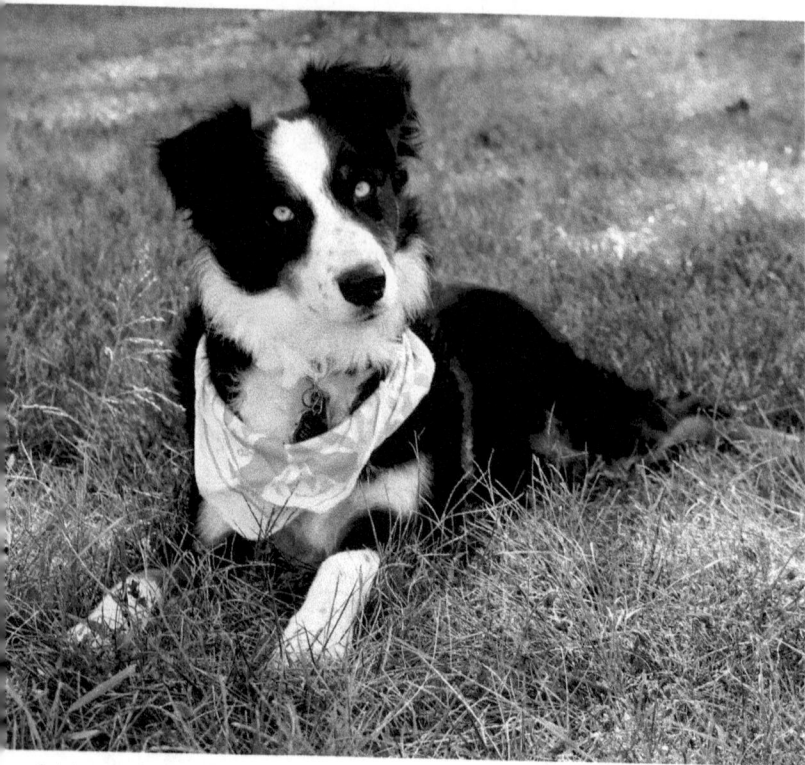

Sabrina–Australian Shepherd

"Trust instinct to the end, even though you can give no reason."

~ Ralph Waldo Emerson

THE DRAGONFLY

I cried today.

I found a dragonfly helpless on the driveway this morning while walking the dog.

As I gently, picked him up, his feet balanced on my left hand. I walked slowly to the grey bench in front of our house and sat.

The dragonfly was in the last stages of life.

His legs yearned for something to grasp. I offered him my robe-covered knee. His lime green translucent wings quivered. I gave him the warmth of my finger, stroking those beautiful wings ever so lightly.

His body, off balance, fell forward. I scooted my soft robe to a more level position to steady him.

His eyes, closing and cloudy, showed pain. With swollen lids, I sobbed for this little dragonfly.

A ragged edge marked the spot where his left lower wing once was. His delicate leafy green body meant for flying and exploring—had been forced to land.

Those sad, cloudy eyes staring up at me were more than I could handle.

I set him down in a safe place under the gray bench and placed a pink Weigela bloom next to the dragonfly. Somehow, I thought if he could still smell the sweetness, it might make his passing a little easier. For one fleeting moment, maybe, he could have peace.

I crawled back into bed, still crying.

"What's wrong honey?" my husband asked.

I explained.

Comforting me with his strong hand in my silky hair, he reminded me about the circle of life. Thoughts overcame me.

It was no accident I was outside on this particular day, at this particular time, walking the dog.

God knew I would be there...to notice the dragonfly and lift him up, gently caressing his broken body, before his journey ended.

I cried today, in awe of God's plan.

The Dragonfly

"...In the tranquil landscape, and especially in the distant line of the horizon, man beholds somewhat as beautiful as his own nature."

~ Ralph Waldo Emerson

BEAUTIFUL BY NATURE

Our last morning on Middle Caicos, hubby and I secured precious time to stroll the long stretch of Mudjin Harbor's beach before heading to another island. The luxurious pink sand on this particular parcel of land caressed our toes with warmth, while aquamarine waves crashed ashore as tempestuous as a lover's first kiss.

As we neared the point where cross breezes blended with the undulating sea's rhythm, aptly-named Dragon Cay came into vision, just offshore. Yesterday, at low tide, we slipped through the shallow water to visit the deserted treasure. Letting out a sigh, I turned slowly clockwise to inhale the breadth and width of nature's majesty in its entire splendor.

Heading back from the beach, we meandered the winding rock path lined with island shrubbery that led to Inspiration Point. High atop a hill, Russell and I rested on the hand-formed coral benches. Sitting side by side, views of the cliffs and the Cay below mesmerized, as the wind tousled our sun-bleached hair. Pink violet clouds performed a whimsical dance across the sky.

I thought about the glimpses of nature encountered during the three days we spent on the island with Sunset Cottage at Blue Horizon Resort as our home base. A sweet creature repeatedly came to mind—the speckled gecko that frequently scurried past us during our walks around the property.

"How do you think the geckos view us humans?"

"Exactly what we would think. Godzilla!"

I chuckled. And almost on cue, a tiny gecko moved gingerly across the brackish grey-white rocks directly in front of me, stopping to perch and observe views of the ocean. That gecko had the right idea.

He spun around, and stared at me, bobbing his head up and down. Sounds weird, but the corners of his mouth upturned into a grin. He blinked his eyes at me once. I wondered if he found me as interesting as I did him.

We sat like this for some time, the two of us studying each other. The little gecko with a natural body of tough outer armor, webbed feet, and curled tale—adaptable to surrounding elements. Me—an outsider in his world of universal beauty.

Looking skyward, an ephemeral sight caught my eye. A sole pelican appeared, gliding, from west to east, dipping and soaring, and crossing our paths for mere seconds—close enough to reach out and touch...

"That's the only pelican we've seen on this leg of the trip."

And the only airborne bird, I thought.

"That's unusual."

Hubby turned to me and smiled.

We sat silent for a few moments on the bench. The turquoise sea between the horizon and offshore lay directly in view.

Beautiful by nature, I thought.

Beautiful by nature...

Beautiful by Nature–Inspiration Point

"Let us be silent, so that we may hear the whisper of God."

~ Ralph Waldo Emerson

RHAPSODY IN CHAIN-LINK

Waiting patiently for my ride at the commuter lot, I eye dozens of birds darting in and out of the cornflower blue Bachelor Buttons. They hop, like Pop Tarts, in and out of the spotty purple poms sprinkled between the parking lot and the outer road. Starlings, grackles and sparrows scamper and fly about. Some walk casually across the pavement.

"Born Again" plays on the Christian radio station. What a joyous June morning—the sun radiant, the wind blowing. The music fits the birds' activity as they gracefully shift in waves like a conductor directing a symphony's string section.

In sharp contrast, a powerline truck business sits across the road. I notice birds, having a heyday, perched atop bucket trucks like they own them! How many birds does it take to start an engine? One? Ten? I chuckle.

Minutes later, they transfer their winged-energy to the next desti- nation—a weathered tree with sparse leaves. Landing on the branches, my feathered friends 'become' the leaves, and I envision a family tree. Just as quickly as the aviators' land, they're off again to roost on the fence's shiny chain-links. The birds' staggered poses and positions create interesting patterns on the fence fabric—similar to notes on a music scale.

Amazing. Several species of social winged-creatures seem to be coexisting side by side. If the grackles, starlings and sparrows could have it their way, the perfect home might be a field of wheat, a meadow of larkspur or a cattail pond.

Instead, harmony is industrial machinery near a commuter park n' ride.

With a melody in my heart, and a song on my lips, these sweet little birds make me smile.

Rhapsody in Chain-Link

*"This time, like all times, is a very good time,
if we but know what to do with it."*

~ Ralph Waldo Emerson

AFTERWORD

In our lifetime, I believe that the places we visit, the people we meet along the way, and the memories we make, shape a person just as the rhythm of the tides shape our infinite coastal shores.

If I could, I'd bundle all my adventures and journeys together—they'd fill the pages of an endless book of life. But for now, I've selected some of my cherished memories for this essay collection.

I've adored the water since I was small child, first discovering the brackish Lake Superior coastline, and months later, the warm waters of Jacksonville Beach, Florida. I remember the first time my Mom plopped me down on a beach; I dug into the sand with my pudgy fingers searching for tiny pebbles and seashells. I scooped those treasures up and placed them in a plastic pink bucket for later observation.

I'm at my best when I'm near water. Nothing compares to lounging in a chair while my toes are submerged in the shallows of the Atlantic, diving with a wild dolphin in the Cayman Islands, or sailing the open ocean.

Water stirs my soul, inspires my mind, and soothes my sometimes, weary bones. Thoughts and ideas spill easily from pen to paper...

I love talking to everyone—especially strangers on the beach. Hearing their stories became an integral part of my memory book—whether it's a Labrador-loving Virginia professor, a North Carolina canine massage therapist, a California cameraman, a young sandcastle builder from the East Coast, or the Kindred Spirit Bench 'keepers'.

If you're outside, you're one with nature. All we need do is look for signs of God's creation—in the yellow cactus flower pushing up through the sand, pelicans soaring overhead, mimosa trees scattered along Southern highways, or a wall dive's gargantuan barrel sponges in hues of magenta.

How could we survive without our pets? The cat that bites only your grey hairs, or the one that lulls you to sleep at night... the big lovable, goofy retriever carrying plastic water bottles, or the boogie-boarding

Newfoundland. Other dogs 'walk themselves' carrying their leads in their mouth. Our pets hog the bed, slobber on our pillow, steal our food, scratch the furniture, give sloppy kisses, chew on shoes...

So, here's my wish for you—travel with wild abandon, appreciate your family and friends while they're alive, get close to nature, notice the little things in life, and hug your fur babies.

Because in the big scheme of things, we're all connected to each other.

Peace, love, and sand dollars,
Sheree

Ocean Rhythms Kindred Spirits is a reminder to be present in the moment, live life with abandon, invariably respecting nature, animals and people.

Join Sheree on a journey as she awakens the wanderlust in her soul, defines moments of clarity while walking on the beach, finds solitude diving with sharks and dolphins, and befriends sea-loving dogs. She'll reveal her strong connection to family and beloved pets, the beauty in a mimosa tree, and the kindred spirit that lives in all of us. A unique essay collection of all things warm and good inspired by the author's love for Emerson.

ABOUT THE AUTHOR

Sheree K. Nielsen is Author/Photographer of 2015 Da Vinci Eye Award Winner, *Folly Beach Dances*, a 'healing' coffee table book inspired by the rhythm of the sea and her lymphoma journey; and coauthor of, *Midnight, The One-Eyed Cat*, a picture book about overcoming handicaps and building confidence.

An award-winning author, poet and photographer, publications include *Long Weekends, Southern Writers Magazine, AAA Southern Traveler, AAA Midwest Traveler, Missouri Life*, magazines, anthologies, newspapers, and websites across the nation and Caribbean.

When not writing, Sheree's usually discovering new beaches and coffeehouses, or checking items off her bucket list with Russell (husband), and two goofy canine kids. Four content cats round out her family on three acres in Missouri.

She has an uncontrollable dependency for dark chocolate.

If you enjoyed *Ocean Rhythms Kindred Spirits*, please let us know your thoughts in the form of a review on Amazon.

CONNECT WITH SHEREE

www.shereenielsen.wordpress.com

Sheree K Nielsen, Author (Facebook)
@ShereeKNielsen (Twitter)
shereenielsen (Instagram)

SHEREE'S OTHER BOOKS

Midnight, The One-Eyed Cat
A charming story of a sweet one-eyed cat who learns to overcome her fears, build her confidence, and find she's okay just as she is, takes children on an inspiring journey into the power of friendship and love. A picture book available on Amazon:

https://www.amazon.com/dp/0996390197

Folly Beach Dances—The Infinite Rhythms of a South Carolina Seashore
What if you could spend a day at the beach, and name it with a dance? A coffee table book of photography and poetry, with reflections by Sheree and Russell Nielsen, and five award-winning women authors. For autographed, gold seal award copies:

www.beachdances.com

@follybeachdance (Twitter)
Folly Beach Dances (Facebook)

https://www.amazon.com/Folly-Beach-Dances-Sheree-Nielsen/dp/0615947131

www.ingramcontent.com/pod-product-compliance
Lightning Source LLC
Chambersburg PA
CBHW072130020426
42334CB00018B/1741